The Mineral Waters Of Indiana

Frt

M

(From the 26th Annual Report of the Department of Geology and Natural Resources of Indiana, 1901.)

...THE...

MINERAL WATERS OF INDIANA

Their Location, Origin and Character.

By W. S. BLATCHLEY.

INDIANAPOLIS:
WM. B. BURFORD, CONTRACTOR FOR STATE PRINTING AND BINDING.
1903.

224496

TN926
.I6B6

W. S. Blatchley

Plate I.

Hotel at LaSalle Springs, Martin County, Indiana.
(See pp. 84, 85.)

THE MINERAL WATERS OF INDIANA.

THEIR LOCATION, ORIGIN AND CHARACTER.

By W. S. Blatchley.

WATER A MINERAL.—A mineral is any natural inorganic compound having a definite chemical composition. Quartz is an example of such a compound. It exists abundantly in nature, and its components are the two elements, silicon and oxygen, in the proportions of 53.3 parts of oxygen to 46.7 of silicon. According to the same definition, water is a mineral. It is very widely distributed in nature and in a pure state is composed of the elements hydrogen and oxygen in the proportions of 11.11 parts of the former to 88.89 of the latter. Pure water, however, is known only in the chemical laboratory, the purest form in nature being the vapor as it rises from ocean, stream or lake. When it condenses and falls as rain or snow, impurities, as carbon dioxide, ammonia, dust, etc., are absorbed from the atmosphere. The water which falls near the close of a long rain, especially in country regions, is almost free from these impurities. Some springs have also nearly pure water; but to separate all foreign matter from it, water must be distilled. Even then it may contain traces of ammonia or other substance which vaporizes at a lower temperature than the water itself.

ORIGIN OF MINERAL WATERS.—Water is the most universal of solvents. Its dissolving power upon rocks, minerals and soils is, however, largely increased by the carbon dioxide which it gathers unto itself while rising and falling through the atmosphere and by the humus acids which it absorbs from the soils. Carbon dioxide, or "carbonic acid," is given out in respiration by all animals and is one of the products of animal and vegetable decay. In this way the supply is constantly being renewed and it becomes distributed through the air and waters. Humus acids are also formed by animal and vegetable decay and occur in all damp soils where such decay is in progress. These acids, when absorbed by the falling or percolating waters, render the latter much more effective in dissolving the rocks with which they come in contact. As the acidulated water penetrates deeper and deeper, it gathers soda and potash from rocks containing feldspar; lime and magnesia from limestones; iron from shales and iron ores; sulphur from gypsum and pyrites, and many other substances from the component rocks with which the slowly percolating water comes in contact. When, therefore, the underground water finally comes to the surface through springs or artesian bores it contains many dissolved solids, gathered during its subterranean wanderings. Among the more common of these are calcium carbonate; salts of iron; magnesium, sodium and potassium carbonates, sulphates or chlorides; calcium chloride; and occasionally, though usually sparingly, aluminum sulphates and lithium salts. It also often contains gases, such as carbonic acid, hydrogen sulphide and nitrogen. The amount and kind of these solid and gaseous ingredients in the issuing water depends wholly upon the kinds of rocks and minerals over which the underground stream has flowed, or through which its component parts have slowly passed. As has been truly said, "the table of contents of a mineral spring is but an index of the various geological strata through which its waters have passed and of the mineral bodies with which they have come in contact." Whatever is soluble in the region through which the underground waters flow will, of course, be taken up by them, and many ingredients are soluble in minute proportions which are usually described as insoluble.

DEFINITION OF "MINERAL WATER."—As water is in itself a mineral, the term "mineral water" is seemingly tautological or redundant. It is a term in common use, but its definition depends largely upon the point of view of the person using it. By the Geologist, the term is usually applied to a water in which the dissolved salts are unusual in quantity or in kind; being present generally in sufficient amount to affect the taste. Since calcium carbonate or "carbonate of lime" is, for the most part, tasteless, the water of a spring or well may contain a large quantity of this common mineral, and yet be termed "pure water" or "hard water," without the prefix "mineral."

The physician and the general public usually give a more restricted definition to the term "mineral water," applying it only to those waters which *are or may be used in the treatment of diseases.* This definition is the one adopted in the present paper, and the waters of the springs and wells mentioned have by experience been proven to possess medicinal properties, or their chemical composition is such as to lead to the supposition that they will prove of value medicinally.

The waters of the majority of the springs described would be classed as "mineral waters" even by the Geologist, since they contain a high percentage of dissolved solids or gaseous materials. On the other hand, a number whose waters have gained much reputation for their curative effects have been found, when analyzed, to hold but a small percentage of mineral matter. Their medicinal value is, however recognized or believed in by the general public. They have come into recognition, probably, through the superior intelligence or energy of their proprietors, who call attention to them in all ways possible. As these owners have more or less capital invested and derive from the springs a revenue, the waters are treated in connection with those which are more highly mineralized. However, they are termed "neutral" or "indifferent" rather than "mineral" in the descriptions which follow.

THE VALUE OF MINERAL WATERS.—Since Dr. Hessler in his paper will give a full discussion of the medicinal value of our mineral waters, but little need be said on this subject. While the person of intelligence, be he physician or be he not, who may visit the various springs, resorts and sanitariums of the State, is soon favorably impressed with their number, the variety of their waters, and, in many instances, the picturesqueness of their surroundings, he at the same time soon comes to smile at the extravagant claims set forth by many of the spring owners and proprietors of sanitariums. The great majority of them assert that the water of their particular spring or well "has no equal in the State," and oftentimes "none on earth." It will cure more diseases than are recognized by the average physician. It is a veritable "fountain of youth"—worthy to be classed with the most famous sought for in the halcyon days of Ponce de Leon.

Such extravagant claims no doubt do much more harm than good. They appeal, for the most part, only to the ignorant. They repel the intelligent invalid and especially the physician who is seeking some spring or sanitarium whose waters and surroundings are especially suited to a case in hand. As Dr. Crook has well said in his excellent work,* "There exists among medical practitioners in the United States a wide-spread skepticism regarding the medicinal value of mineral waters. This incredulity is no doubt based, to a considerable extent, upon a somewhat justifiable prejudice; but may it not be due, in a much greater degree, to a want of correct information? We are all acquainted with the mineral spring advertising circular. It comes to us clothed in a respectable, even elegant dress; but it too frequently portrays the virtues of the alleged healing fluid which it represents in language of absurd hyperbole. When the intelligent practitioner reads that a certain water is positively curative in an imposing list of diseases, as set forth in divers pages of testi-

---

*"The Mineral Waters of the United States and Their Therapeutic Uses," p. 34.

monials from renovated statesmen, restored clergymen and rejuvenated old ladies, and then learns from the analysis that it contains two or three grains of lime-salts to the gallon, with the remaining ingredients requiring perhaps a third or fourth decimal figure to express, he can hardly be blamed for tossing the circular into his wastebasket, with an objurgation upon quacks generally and the mineral spring quack in particular; yet the conservative physician will find a safe and dignified position between that of the pretentious advertisement which claims everything and that of the medical skeptic who will believe nothing."

It is a well recognized fact among physicians that too little water is used by most persons. Pure water, when taken in quantity, is in itself beneficial. It flushes the channels of the body, and by increasing the liquid portion of the blood, aids materially in bearing the food particles to the absorbents and in carrying away the harmful products of the excretory organs. Especially is hot water valuable, not only by acting as a tonic, but by causing an increased activity of heart, lungs, skin and kidneys. This stimulation of the more important organs brings about better nutrition, which in turn causes more and better blood to be sent to all the organs. The beneficial action of pure or "neutral" waters upon the system as a whole is thus accounted for, and in general it may be said that a person can drink *ad libitum* of such waters, and receive only benefit therefrom.

When the water contains chemicals or mineral ingredients which are known to be remedies for certain diseases, its importance as a medicinal agent is thereby increased. Each of the common minerals found in solution in such waters has a distinct effect upon some organ of the body when taken in quantity. No one of them or no combination of them is a "cure all" as claimed by so many of the advertising circulars sent out. The average person knows but little concerning the medicinal or remedial effects of the mineral compounds found in such waters. He should, therefore, if suffering from a well-defined disease, always consult a reputable physician before using freely any strong mineral water, else the result may be in the highest degree harmful rather than beneficial. The physician can judge from the chemical analysis and from his general knowledge of medicine the curative value of any water for the disease in hand. For this reason an accurate chemical analysis is one of the best advertisements which the proprietor of any mineral water resort can place before the public. It is far better for such proprietor, after having such analysis made, to learn from a good physician the exact curative properties of the water, and then advertise them judiciously

and truthfully, at the same time calling attention to the attractiveness of the surroundings and advantages for recreation, rather than
claim, as is so often done, that the water is a universal panacea for
all diseases to which humanity is subject.

It is the writer's opinion, based on personal experience, that the
change of surroundings and diet, the increased amount of recreation
and exercise, obtained by a few weeks spent at the sanitariums and
resorts, have quite as much to do with bringing about a cure of many
patients as does the water itself. There are many ordinary springs
of pure water, i. e., water containing only a few grains of lime or
iron salts per gallon, located near villages in this State, which are
claimed by the inhabitants to possess remarkable curative properties.
Old persons who seldom get ten rods from their homes, and business
men who are kept indoors most of their time, begin to visit such
springs, and once or twice a week walk or drive quite a distance to
bring home a jug full of the water. The increased amount of exercise
thus obtained, as well as the change of scenery, however limited,
and perhaps the drinking of an extra amount of water each day, are
the causes of the improved health rather than any curative properties
possessed by the water. The psychic agency in the cure of disease
is a powerful one and in no instance should it be neglected. A change
of place, of surroundings, if possible of climate, is for a time, to the
person "run down" in general health, almost always beneficial. Facilities for recreation, as bathing, fishing, bowling, etc., in connection
with a sanitarium, lend much to its value by furnishing a means of
exercise which will aid to keep the thoughts of the patient from
dwelling too much upon himself and his ailments, fancied or real.

*"Curæ vacuus hunc adeas locum
ut morborum vacuus abire queas"*

was the inscription above the baths of Antoninus at Rome. "Come
to this place free from care that you may leave it free from disease,"
is a maxim as much to be regarded at present as in the palmy days
of the Roman empire.

CLASSIFICATION OF INDIANA MINERAL WATERS.—Many elaborate
schemes of classification of mineral waters have, in the past, been
put forward by different writers. One of the most simple, based upon
the chemical ingredients of the water, is that of Dr. A. C. Peale, of
the United States Geological Survey. According to this classification, the mineral waters of Indiana may be grouped under the following heads:

I.—Alkaline.

II.—Saline.

III.—Chalybeate.

IV.—Neutral or Indifferent.

Class I.—*The alkaline waters* include those whose principal mineral ingredients are the *carbonates* of one or more of the following elements: calcium, magnesium, potassium and sodium. The majority of the Indiana waters of this group contain calcium carbonate (carbonate of lime) or magnesium carbonate, as the principal salt. Oftentimes both are present in quantity. While frequent in the drift-covered area and along the outcrops of the limestone districts of southern, central and southeastern Indiana, the springs and wells containing the waters of this class are far less noted for their medicinal virtues than are those of the next group.

Class II.—*The saline waters* include the large majority of the mineral waters of Indiana now in use. In the waters of this class the *sulphates* or *chlorides* of calcium, magnesium, aluminum, potassium or sodium form the principal salts in solution. Sodium chloride (common salt) is the most common ingredient of this class of waters, though magnesium sulphate (Epsom salt) or sodium sulphate (Glauber's salt) occur in most of the waters of the group. Where these two salts occur in quantity such waters may be designated as *sulphated* and purgative. The springs of Clark, Floyd and Brown counties, described on subsequent pages, which issue from the New Providence shale at the base of the Knobstone formation, produce excellent examples of saline waters rich in the sulphates of magnesium and sodium. These waters resemble closely in chemical composition, taste and medicinal effect the celebrated Hungarian water, known as the Hunyadi Janos. Their salts are derived from the ingredients found in the New Providence shale. It is probable that many additional springs producing water similar to those described, exist in the counties where this shale outcrops.

Aluminum sulphate is found in a number of the "bitter springs" in the coal regions of southwestern Indiana, notably in Gibson, Pike and Warrick counties. It is derived from the shales overlying the coal veins or from the pyrites accompanying them. The sulphur of the pyrites or iron sulphide, when exposed to air or water, takes up oxygen and forms sulphuric acid. This in turn combines with the alumina of the shale to form aluminum sulphate. A portion of the sulphuric acid may also combine with the iron to form iron or ferric sulphate, which is also often one of the ingredients of these "bitter springs." When such sulphate is present the water may be termed a *saline-chalybeate* water.

When the carbonates of the metals mentioned in *Class I* are found in quantity in the same water with the sulphates or chlorides of *Class II*, the water may be termed *alkaline-saline*.

Class III.—*The chalybeate waters.* To this group belong the waters of all springs and wells having *salts of iron* in solution. Chalybeate or iron springs probably occur in every county in Indiana, though but few of them have been developed for commercial purposes. Iron carbonate, like carbonate of lime, is slightly soluble in rain water or water containing carbonic acid in solution. Iron carbonate is found throughout the clay deposits of the drift-covered area of the State and in many of the shales of the driftless area of the southern portion. The underground waters, when they come in contact with this carbonate, dissolve a small portion of it and form an iron bi-carbonate. On coming to the surface, either in springs or wells, this bicarbonate gives up the carbonic acid and absorbs oxygen. It is thus changed into iron oxide, which precipitates or settles as a brownish yellow sediment. This is seen in and alongside the rills bearing water away from the springs, as well as in the springs themselves. In the country these are commonly called "sulphur springs," though their waters contain no sulphate or sulphide, nor have they the least trace of the odor of hydrogen sulphide.

According to Dr. Crook, "These bi-carbonated chalybeate waters ars usually most valuable for internal administration. Not only does carbonic acid increase the solubility of the iron, but it disguises its otherwise astringent and ferruginous taste, and aids in its speedy absorption and assimilation. These waters prove of great value in cases of anæmia or poverty of the blood. Clinical experience has shown that they cause an increase in the appetite, a return to the normal color, a gain in weight and strength, and a general improvement of the bodily functions. It matters not though the iron be present in small quantities, and few of the carbonated iron waters contain more than five or six grains per gallon. The blood contains normally about forty-five grains of iron, and this quantity can not be permanently increased by consuming large quantities. It is probable that the deficiency, no matter how produced, never exceeds fifteen or twenty grains. A chalybeate water containing not more than one grain to the gallon will speedily show its influence in the returning color and increased tone and vigor of the system."

While chalybeate springs are found in numbers in almost every county in the State, but few of them are mentioned in the present

2—Geol.

paper as the time at the disposal of the writer forbade him visiting only a few of those which are undeveloped. Their waters can be taken with freedom by most persons, since they are readily assimilated and comparatively devoid of taste. After a short use they are generally relished and preferred to the waters of the purer springs with which they are usually found associated. Many of the larger springs producing chalybeate waters will, in the future, doubtless be utilized as resorts and will well repay the capital invested in their development.

Class IV.—*Neutral* or *indifferent* waters have been already referred to. They contain such a small quantity of mineral matter as to be excluded from either of the above named classes, and yet have been utilized for medicinal purposes and are highly recommended by some physicians. Those so utilized and described in the present paper are mentioned specifically as "neutral" in the text. Many of the so-called "potable water" or "pure water" springs of the State are as worthy of development for medicinal purposes as those described. Proper advertising and the expenditure of some capital in furnishing means of recreation is about all that is necessary to make of them noted health resorts.

HYDROGEN SULPHIDE AS AN INGREDIENT OF MINERAL WATER.— Many of the more important mineral springs and artesian wells of Indiana emit with their water an ill-smelling gas known as hydrogen sulphide or sulphuretted hydrogen. It is usually mentioned as having the odor and taste of rotten eggs, since it is formed in quantity in such eggs during the process of decay. This gas is found in such quantity in some of the mineral waters as to destroy or disguise the taste of the other minerals present, and therefore to render the water nauseating or unpalatable. It is formed in the earth by a chemical process in which the sulphur of calcium sulphide or gypsum is replaced by the hydrogen of water according to the formula

$$CaS + H_2O = CaO + H_2S.$$

As the water issues through spring or well much of the gas escapes, permeating the surrounding atmosphere with its characteristic odor. When brought in contact with the oxygen of the air the gas is often disassociated or split up into its elements. The sulphur is deposited as a white or whitish-yellow sediment upon surrounding objects while the hydrogen joins with the oxygen to form water. The name "white-sulphur" is often given to the spring or well where such deposit is formed. Again, when salts of iron are present, this sulphur, when set free, may unite with the iron to form black flakes of iron sulphide, which settle slowly to the bottom of spring or rill.

Various opinions are held by physicians as to the medicinal value of hydrogen sulphide. It is poisonous when inhaled and when thus taken into the system in quantity is quickly fatal. Its medicinal virtues, when taken into the stomach, are fully discussed on a subsequent page by Dr. Hessler. On account of its gaseous form and its consequent rapid escape when exposed to air, the quantity in any mineral water is variable. The presence of the gas in sufficient quantity to make its presence known by odor or taste, usually causes the name "sulphur water" to be given locally to the water issuing from a spring or well. In the descriptions which follow the term "sulphuretted" is used to donate its presence. Thus "saline-sulphuretted" indicates a water belonging to Class II, which contains hydrogen sulphide. The waters of the springs of Orange and Martin counties, as well as those of the artesian wells at Shelbyville, Martinsville, Spencer, Montezuma, and many other places, are thus designated as "saline-sulphuretted."

SPRINGS IN GENERAL.—The mineral waters of Indiana are derived from both springs and wells. In early days that of the springs alone was used, but now artesian and other wells producing such water exceed in number the natural springs.

What is the cause of a spring? Why does water issue forth from a certain point on a hillside, or well up from a certain place in a valley? These are questions which every person interested in nature has probably asked many times. In answer it may be said that the water falling as rain on any land area in a given time may be divided into three parts, viz.: (a) That which rushes immediately down the slopes and causes the floods of streams and rivers. (b) That which sinks slowly into the earth, where for a time it does much work in dissolving rocks and forming soils; and then finally reappears as springs and forms the regular supply of streams and rivers. (c) That which sinks still deeper and never appears again on the surface, but finds its way by underground channels into the ocean, or else is added to the permanent supply of water which by deep borings we know exists at great depths below the land surface.

The amount of water which sinks below the surface to form springs depends largely upon the character of the surface. Where this is bare of trees and other vegetation that which flows directly off is much greater in quantity than where the soil is covered with vegetation. The roots of trees, shrubs and herbs, the stems of moss and grass, dead twigs, leaves and other rubbish, all retard the flow of water and so give time for more of it to enter the soil and sink slowly until it reaches an impervious stratum of clay or rock. It is a well known fact that while the annual rainfall in Indiana has been almost the same for the past forty years, the size of the springs and streams has slowly decreased. Many of the former, in existence a half century ago, have wholly disappeared, while the flow from others has diminished fully one-half. Since the water supply of streams, especially during times of drought, is dependent wholly upon springs, many streams which once had a large flow in summer are now wholly dry for several months. The cause of this is, without doubt, the clearing away of the forests which, with the artificial drainage of the cleared land, allows the rapid removal of the rainfall. The water, which formerly sank slowly beneath the surface and more slowly seeped out through many springs, is now carried away in a day or two in floods which often leave ruin and desolation in their wake.

Wherever underground water appears at the surface, on the side or at the foot of a hill, or bubbles up from a natural opening in a valley, such an appearance is termed a *spring.* The surface water, in sinking, penetrates the soil and the porous strata, as sand, gravel, sandstone, etc., beneath, until it reaches an impervious layer of clay, shale or limestone through which it can not pass. It flows along the surface of this impervious layer, sometimes for miles, until it finds an opening on the face or at the foot of a bluff, or in the bank of a lake or pool, from which it issues as a spring. The largest springs usually issue from fissures in the rock, or bubble up through a cavity in a valley or bed of a stream. Their water has passed along a porous stratum probably for a great distance, and has been prevented from rising by the overlying impervious stratum and from sinking by a similar underlying stratum. As it reaches a fissure it immediately rises, being forced up by the great hydrostatic pressure behind it, until it wells or bubbles out above the surface. In the limestone regions of southern Indiana there are numbers of these "fissure springs," some of which are large enough to be utilized for water power in running mills. One of the most noted of these is Harrison Spring, a few miles west of Corydon. This wells up in a valley with sufficient flow and force to run both a grist and a saw mill. Another, a few miles east of Mitchell, Lawrence County, issues from a cave with great force and was long utilized for power in a grist mill and a distillery.

As already noted, the subterranean water dissolves, during its flow, portions of the rocks with which it comes in contact. If these be of the proper character and the distance in underground flow be great enough, it will issue as "mineral water," and the spring be termed a "mineral spring." Since for ages the water bearing the salts dissolved from the different rocks in the solid crust of the earth has been flowing into the ocean, the latter may be termed the great mineral spring of the world. About three and a quarter per cent. of its waters consist of soluble salts thus derived from the rocks of the land. These salts are, for the most part, the same as exist in many of the noted "mineral springs" now in existence; namely, sodium chloride, magnesium sulphate, sodium sulphate, calcium carbonate, etc. However, many more varieties of salts exist in the ocean than in any other mineral spring on earth.

If the different strata through which the slowly sinking water flows be principally sand, gravel, limestone or sandstone, the issuing water will be "pure" or "potable," since the materials mentioned contain little soluble matter other than carbonate of lime or salts of iron. The great majority of springs in the northern part of the State where the drift area exists are of this nature. Many of them contain iron bi-carbonate in sufficient quantity to be termed "chalybeate springs," and it is possible that analyses would show their waters to be similar to those of many of the "iron springs" of noted health resorts.

OCCURRENCE OF MINERAL WATER IN DEEP WELLS.—But a few deep bores were sunk in Indiana previous to 1886, when natural gas in commercial quantities was first discovered in the State. Several of the bores put down before that date, notably those at Reelsville, Putnam County; Terre Haute, Vigo County; Lodi, Fountain County, and at two or three localities in Crawford County, had developed artesian flows of mineral water, but at only one of these wells was this water used to any extent for medicinal purposes, notwithstanding that the analyses of the water from most of the wells were made and published in the older reports of this Department, and were copied quite extensively in the medical journals and works on mineral waters.

Since 1886 more than 14,000 deep bores have been sunk for oil and gas in different parts of the State. Of these a number developed flowing water; while in a still larger number the water rose within easy pumping distance of the surface. In the different strata encountered above the Trenton limestone, especially outside of the main oil and gas fields as at present defined, large supplies of excellent potable water were often found. In most instances this occurred in the Niagara limestone; was cased off, and the bore sunk to the Trenton limestone, where salt water was found. By plugging the well between the potable and the salt water the former has been made available as a source of water supply for many cities and towns or for manufacturing and other industries.

The output of a number of the flowing wells in central and western Indiana proved to be a saline-sulphuretted mineral water of high value as a medicinal agent. Such water is now being utilized in sanitariums at Greenwood, Martinsville, Columbus, Gosport, Spencer, Terre Haute, Montezuma and other localities; while in a number of places wells are producing a water as valuable, but which is being used only locally. In many of the deep bores, two or three different veins of mineral water were struck. The Niagara limestone furnishes most of the saline-sulphuretted water now in use. The water of the Trenton limestone and the underlying St. Peter's sandstone is, in most instances, too brackish, i. e., contains too large a percentage of common salt for medicinal use; though in a few cases a fair quality of "blue lick" water, containing magnesium sulphate in quantity and also much sulphuretted hydrogen, is found in the St. Peter's sandstone.

In general it may be said that the waters of the deep wells contain a much larger percentage of mineral matter than those of the springs and shallow wells. This is due to the fact that the deeper subterranean waters are in direct contact with the rocks which yield them the salts a much longer time, since the water is not so soon renewed as that in springs which have a constant flow. It is probable, also, that more or less sea water was left in the Niagara and Trenton limestones and in the St. Peter's and Potsdam sandstones, at the time of the recession of the ocean, from the area now occupied by these formations. The mineral contents of this sea water have there remained for ages, and only when furnished a vent by artificial boring does the hydrostatic pressure behind force it upward as an artesian flow of so-called "mineral water." As impervious strata of rock, shale, etc., usually exist between the surface and the source of the mineral water in the deep bores, it follows that the supply of water can not be renewed by percolation as in ordinary springs. Dr. Edward Orton, of Ohio, proved that the hydrostatic pressure behind the salt water, gas and oil of the Trenton limestone of Indiana is caused by the waters of Lake Superior. The level of this lake is 600 feet above tide level, and by adding this height to the number of feet at which the Trenton lies below tide level and calculating the pressure on this basis he found that it corresponded closely with the original rock pressure of gas, oil or salt water. The ultimate source of the mineral water which rises from great depths in the different artesian bores of the State is probably accounted for in the same manner, i. e., it comes from lakes which lie far distant from the point at which it wells forth. During its long journey it has plenty of time to gain, both by solution and chemical action, the large percentage of mineral salts which it holds.

CHEMICAL ANALYSES.—The means at command forbade the making of but few analyses of mineral waters especially for this paper. The analyses incorporated are, for the most part, those which had already been made for the owners of the various springs and wells. A number of these have already been published in former reports of this Department. In every case, but one or two, the name of the chemist making the analysis is known and given.

The results of the analyses, as furnished, were expressed in many different ways. These have been reduced to a common standard, viz., grains per U. S. gallon of 231 cubic inches, as that was thought to be the most intelligible to the greatest number of people. "Everyone is acquainted with the familiar gallon measure, which equals eight wine pints. With the quantitative analysis before us and a knowledge of the capacity of the vessel from which the patient drinks, we can make, under any circumstances, a fairly close estimate of the amount of mineral water which he is taking. With the exception of a few very strong springs, concerning which specific instructions should always be given, it is not necessary to be absolutely exact in the dosage of mineral waters, and if the patient should imbibe a gill or two more or less than the amount prescribed, no harm is done." The gases, hydrogen sulphide and carbon dioxide, when expressed in grains, have also been reduced to cubic inches.

The conversions from the form as furnished into grains per U. S. gallon, or into cubic inches, of the gases mentioned, was made according to the following table:

Parts per   100,000 × .583 = Grains per U. S. gallon.
Parts per 1,000,000 × .058 = Grains per U. S. gallon.
Grains per imperial gallon × .833 = Grains per U. S. gallon.
One grain of hydrogen sulphide = 2.596 cubic inches.
One grain of carbon dioxide = 2.006 cubic inches.

ALLEN COUNTY.

ABBOTT MAGNETIC MINERAL WELL.

WATER = *Alkaline-saline-sulphuretted.*

LOCATION.—Two miles southeast of the courthouse at Fort Wayne, a city of 47,000 population, situated at the junction of the St. Joseph, Maumee and St. Mary's rivers; 148 miles east of Chicago, 117 miles northeast of Indianapolis, and 94 miles southwest of Toledo. Seven railways enter the city, furnishing ample transportation facilities in all directions.

ORIGIN AND CHARACTER OF THE WATER.—The well which yields the mineral water was sunk for gas in 1888. It is located rather unfortunately, being one mile distant from street car lines, and near railroad yards. The total depth of the well was 1,900 feet. The mineral water was found in the Trenton limestone and rose only to within 900 feet of the surface. The water was analyzed by Dr. Charles R. Dryer, with the following result:

ANALYSIS OF WATER FROM ABBOTT WELL, FORT WAYNE, INDIANA.

	Grains per U. S. Gallon.
Sodium chloride (NaCl)	2,993.793
Magnesium chloride (MgCl$_2$)	148.825
Magnesium sulphate (MgSO$_4$)	143.283
Calcium sulphate (CaSO$_4$)	20.71
Calcium carbonate (CaCO$_3$)	597.401
Potassium bromide (KBr)	5.469
Ferrous carbonate (FeCO$_3$)	21.119
Silica, alumina and organic matter	43.755
Nitrates and phosphates	traces
Total solids	3,974.355

Gases.	Cu. In. per Gal.
Carbon dioxide (CO$_2$)	2.31
Hydrogen sulphide (H$_2$S)	2.3677

A sanitarium and bath house for the utilization of the water was erected and for a few years was well patronized, and the water achieved quite a renown in the cure of rheumatism, skin diseases and nervous troubles. In time, however, difficulties arose in pumping the water from so great a depth, and the place was abandoned. It has recently come into the possession of Louis Fox, a wealthy citizen of Fort Wayne, who proposes to reopen it as a sanitarium on a larger scale. The water is said to possess magnetic qualities to such an extent that a knife held in it for a few seconds will pick up a nail or other article of iron or steel. Hence the name "Magnetic Mineral Well."

BARTHOLOMEW COUNTY.

THE COLUMBUS SANITARIUM CO.

WATER = Saline-sulphuretted.

LOCATION.—In the environs of Columbus, the county seat, a city of 8,500 population, situated 40 miles south of Indianapolis, and 69 miles north of Louisville.

The city possesses all modern improvements and is reached by three branches of the Pennsylvania Railway, and from Cincinnati and points east by the Columbus and Greensburg Division of the "Big Four" Railway. Electric street cars pass within one block of the sanitarium. A rich agricultural region surrounds the city, affording facilities for pleasant country driving.

ORIGIN AND CHARACTER OF WATER.—The water used in the sanitarium of this company is from an artesian well located near the northern limits of the city of Columbus. This well was sunk in 1893 to a depth of 1,700 feet. The water now in use was struck, according to Dr. M. N. Elrod, in the Waldron shale at a depth of about 180 feet. The sulphur in the water is probably derived from iron pyrites in this shale. The water was cased off until after the well was proven barren of both gas and oil, when it was allowed to flow. The well is in a strip of low ground 300 feet northwest of the main building of the sanitarium. In November, 1901, the flow was but about two gallons a minute to a height of about three feet above the surface. It has been demonstrated by the city engineer of Columbus that the water can be forced by the artesian pressure 200 feet above its source. For use in the sanitarium the water is pumped into tanks located above the boiler house near the sanitarium, and from these tanks flows into the bath rooms. The water has a constant temperature of 56° F. as it issues from the well. The odor of hydrogen sulphide is distinct but not strong. The water has a rather agreeable, sweetish-saline taste and when fresh from the well is clear and sparkling.

Its analysis by Dr. J. N. Hurty, of Indianapolis, resulted as follows:

ANALYSIS OF MINERAL WATER FROM ARTESIAN WELL, COLUMBUS, INDIANA.

	Grains per U. S. Gallon.
Calcium carbonate ($CaCO_3$)	6.786
Magnesium carbonate ($MgCO_3$)	8.447
Sodium chloride (NaCl)	37.947
Calcium sulphate ($CaSO_4$)	3.501
Sodium sulphate (Na_2SO_4)	5.136
Magnesium chloride ($MgCl_2$)	0.437
Alumina (Al_2O_3)	2.203
Silica (SiO_2)	0.443
Total solids	64.900

Hydrogen sulphide (H_2S) 4.031 cubic inches per gallon.

For the depth from which the water is obtained the percentage of solid ingredients is not large, but the water is well suited for sanitary baths, the use to which it is principally put. It is claimed by the proprietors to be especially efficacious in diseases of the skin and kidneys, rheumatism, gout, neurasthenia, etc. It is bottled and sold on the market, but as yet the sale has been limited. It is a mild saline water and may be used freely.

IMPROVEMENTS.—The sanitarium in which the Columbus artesian water is principally used, was first opened in August, 1894, and until 1900 was operated only as a sanitarium and bath house without hotel accommodations. In the latter year a twenty-room hotel was constructed on the same lot. The sanitarium is open during the entire year and is well equipped for giving mineral and vapor baths, there being ten bath rooms with attendants. Competent consulting physicians reside in the building and furnish advice to all patients.

THE AZALIA MINERAL SPRING.

WATER = *Chalybeate.*

LOCATION.—Quite a number of chalybeate or iron springs exist in Bartholomew County. The best known is the "Azalia Mineral Spring," located six miles southeast of Columbus, on the land of Nathan H. Newsom, southeast quarter Section 16 (8 N., 6 E.), near the junction of Brush and Little Sand Creeks. The nearest railway station is Elizabethtown, on the Madison Branch of the Pennsylvania Railway, two miles east.

ORIGIN AND CHARACTER OF WATER.—The water bubbles up at the rate of about two gallons per minute through the sand, and probably through a fissure in the underlying rock. The temperature is 53° F. The water has a very decided taste of iron which probably issues as the bi-carbonate and is changed to the peroxide on contact with air. Lime and magnesia are also present in the form of bi-carbonates, but not in larger quantity than in most other spring and well waters of the vicinity. The spring is surrounded by a fine growth of elm and other forest trees, and is a noted resort for picnic and pleasure parties. There is little doubt but that a successful sanitarium for invalids afflicted with diseases for which chalybeate water is beneficial, could be established at this place.

Another chalybeate spring of more than local repute, and possessing a much larger flow of water, wells up through a fissure in the limestone just below the Anderson Falls on Fall Fork Creek.

BROWN COUNTY.

McCARTY'S MINERAL SPRING.

WATER = *Saline-sulphated* (Purgative).

LOCATION.—The spring which yields the mineral water sold under the name of "Blue Mountain Laxine" is located near the postoffice of Mount Moriah, in the northeastern part of Brown County, near the Bartholomew County line. It is on the land of W. H. McCarty, southeast quarter Section 5 (9 N., 4 E.), about 12 miles northwest of Columbus and half way between Edinburg, Johnson County, and Nashville, Brown County. The nearest railway station is Taylorsville, nine miles east on the Louisville Division of the Pennsylvania Railway, 35 miles south of Indianapolis.

ORIGIN AND CHARACTER OF THE WATER.—The spring is located at the base of a hill or bluff of Knobstone about 35 rods from the postoffice of Mount Moriah. The water comes up through a dark blue mud and has an estimated flow of about eight gallons per hour. The spring is walled up with sawed stone, but no other improvements have been made.

The water was used locally by the owner and his neighbors for stomach and kidney troubles for some years and about 1887 was placed on sale at Franklin and other towns. It gained slowly in reputation until 1900, when Dr. J. L. Morris, of the Columbus, Indiana, sanitarium leased the spring for ten years and had an analysis of the water made by T. W. Smith, of Indianapolis, which resulted as follows:

ANALYSIS OF "BLUE MOUNTAIN LAXINE WATER" FROM MOUNT MORIAH, BROWN COUNTY, INDIANA.

	Grains per U. S. Gallon.
Sodium chloride (NaCl)	15.28
Calcium sulphate (CaSO₄)	8.40
Magnesium sulphate (MgSO₄)	325.30
Sodium sulphate (Na₂SO₄)	319.92
Silica (SiO₂)	55.29
Iron	trace
Total solids	724.19

The water is clear and sparkling and has no odor, but possesses the bitter taste characteristic of its two main constituents—Epsom salt and Glauber's salt. In composition and taste it closely resembles the saline waters of Clark County, described on subsequent pages, and probably gains its chemical constituents from the same source, viz., the New Providence shale, which forms the base of the Knobstone. It is an aperient or cathartic, depending on the dose. The percentage of free silicia is surprisingly large. The water is now being hauled overland to the Columbus sanitarium, where it is used and where it is also bottled and placed on the market. About twenty barrels were sold in 1901 at an average price of 30 cents a gallon.

NASHVILLE ARTESIAN WELLS.

WATER = *Saline-sulphuretted* (?).

LOCATION.—In the northwest quarter of the northwest quarter of Section 19 (9 N., 3 E.), within the corporate limits of Nashville, the county seat, a town of 400 population, situated near the center of the county.

ORIGIN AND CHARACTER OF THE WATER.—Two wells drilled in 1899; one on the public square, a short distance southwest of the court house, to a depth of 500 feet, yielded for a time a good flow of water, which ceased when the second well was drilled. The latter, two squares south of the court house, was drilled to a depth of 530 feet, and when turned on full-force, flows about ten gallons of mineral water per minute, which has a temperature of 56° F.

The water is clear and sparkling with hydrogen sulphide and carbonic acid gases. It has an agreeable saline-sulphur taste, and is much used by the citizens of Nashville and vicinity. It is diuretic and laxative in effect and, when taken in quantity, purgative. No analysis has been made.

IMPROVEMENTS.—A frame hotel and bath house, known as the "Nashville Sanitarium," containing 24 rooms, was erected in 1900, and is open to guests from June to November of each year. The water is piped into the house, and is used for both drinking and bathing, there being six well equipped bath rooms. Up to the present, the guests have been mostly from Brown and adjacent counties. With better means of transportation afforded, there is little doubt but that the number of guests would largely increase, as the water appears to be of excellent quality.

CARROLL COUNTY.

DELPHI ARTESIAN WELL.

WATER = *Saline-sulphuretted.*

LOCATION.—Two squares south of the court house at Delphi, a city of 2,300 inhabitants, located at the junction of the C., I. & L. (Monon) and Wabash railways, 72 miles northwest of Indianapolis and 112 miles southeast of Chicago. Delphi is picturesquely located on the high banks of Deer Creek, near the junction of that stream and the Wabash River. It is situated in a region replete with fine roads and romantic scenery, so that the facilities for driving and enjoyment of out of door exercise are excellent.

ORIGIN AND CHARACTER OF THE WATER.—The well which yields the artesian flow of mineral water was one of several put down in and around Delphi about 1890, in search of oil and gas. It was sunk on the north bank of Deer Creek to a depth of 912 feet. It developed a strong vein of mineral water, a slight flow of gas and a trace of oil. It was shot with nitroglycerin in an endeavor to increase the flow of gas, but failed to do so. However, gas has continued to issue with the water and in August, 1901, when set on fire, would burn steadily with a flame reaching a foot or two from the end of the escape pipe.

The water was analyzed by Dr. J. N. Hurty, of Indianapolis, who reported on it as follows:

ANALYSIS OF WATER FROM ARTESIAN WELL AT DELPHI, INDIANA.

	Grains per U. S. Gallon.
Calcium carbonate ($CaCO_3$)	0.708
Magnesium chloride ($MgCl_2$)	1.678
Sodium chloride (NaCl)	30.885
Potassium chloride (KCl)	0.023
Calcium sulphate ($CaSO_4$)	0.004
Iron and aluminum oxides (Fe_2O_3&Al_2O_3)	0.058
Total	33.356

Sulphuretted hydrogen (H_2S), 7.76 cubic inches per gallon.

"This water may be classed with the best known salt sulphur mineral waters. In rheumatism and all indigestion troubles and all strumous diseases, it will be found a sovereign remedy. It will be found best for drinking if diluted with an equal amount of pure water, but for baths it may be used without dilution, although in some instances dilution would be advantageous."—*Hurty.*

The water flows at the rate of about six gallons per minute and has a temperature of 57° F. It has the distinctive odor and taste of hydrogen sulphide, with just enough of that of common salt to make it palatable.

A sanitarium and bath house was established in connection with the well in 1893, and ran for several years. Litigation involving the title of the property and poor management, finally caused its closing. The water was also shipped quite extensively for a time. At present it is free to everybody and is much used by the residents of Delphi. The Commercial Club of the city believe strongly in the medical virtues of the water and will encourage and lend assistance to any one who will undertake the erection of a new sanitarium.

A second well, producing a smaller flow of the same water, is located on the south side of Deer Creek, within a few hundred yards of the one above described.

CASS COUNTY.

LOGANSPORT ARTESIAN WELLS.

WATER == Saline-sulphuretted.

LOCATION.—Two wells. one the "West End well," near the crossing of the Vandalia and Pennsylvania railways, one and a fourth miles southwest of the court house; the other, the "Water Works well," on the south bank of Eel River near the city water works. Logansport is a city of 17,000 population, located 120 miles southeast of Chicago, on the Pennsylvania, Vandalia and Wabash railways.

ORIGIN AND CHARACTER OF THE WATER.—Two wells sunk for gas struck mineral water in the Trenton limestone at about 1,100 feet. The West End well produced quite a flow of water for a number of years, but was finally plugged. The flow can be renewed at any time by removing the plug. An analysis of the water from this well was made some years ago by Floyd Davis, Iowa State Chemist, who reported on it as follows:

ANALYSIS OF WATER FROM WEST END ARTESIAN WELL, LOGANSPORT, INDIANA.

Grains per U. S. Gallon.

Sodium chloride (NaCl)	792.716
Magnesium chloride (MgCl)	78.570
Magnesium sulphate (MgSO₄)	46.884
Calcium sulphate (CaSO₄)	104.494
Calcium carbonate (CaCO₃)	107.109
Silica (SiO₂)	4.460
Total	1134.233

"Besides the above, traces of potassium chloride and alumina were present. This is a very strong saline water, its active constituents being sodium chloride, magnesium chloride and magnesium sulphate."

The sodium chloride promotes tissue changes generally and is of use in dyspepsia with deficient acidity; the magnesium salts are aperient, in sufficient doses laxative or cathartic, and are useful in eliminating waste products and in keeping the bowels regular. The calcium carbonate is an antacid, serviceable in excessive acidity of the stomach, and it also acts as a diuretic.

This water is especially indicated in uric acid, gouty and rheumatic conditions.

The Water Works well, in 1901, was flowing about three gallons per minute of a clear water, which had the odor and taste of hydrogen sulphide, combined with the bitter taste of magnesium sulphate. The water rises four feet above the surface and flows from a small discharge pipe, with a temperature of 56° F. It is used to some extent locally. No analysis was available.

CLARK COUNTY.

KING'S MINERAL SPRING.

WATER = Saline-sulphated (Purgative).

LOCATION.—On the southwest quarter of Section 233, Illinois Grant, near the northeast corner of Carr Township, Clark County, one and a half miles north of Wilson's Switch, the nearest railway station, on the C., I. & L. (Monon) Railway, 18 miles north of Louisville, 305 miles south of Chicago. Postoffice, Dallas.

ORIGIN AND CHARACTER OF THE WATER.—A spring, which in its natural state issued from the side of a bluff of shale, has been dug out to a depth of six feet and walled with stone. It has an output of about 15 gallons per hour, of a clear water, without odor, but with a very bitter taste, the water being strongly impregnated with mineral salts derived by leaching through the New Providence shale. This shale is one of the lower members of the Knobstone formation, which comprises a large portion of the surface of Clark, Scott, Jackson and other counties of this portion of Indiana. It is a fine, greenish-gray, marly shale that pulverizes when dry without difficulty. This shale is the source of all but one of the springs of mineral water described from Clark County, as well as the one from Floyd County.

An analysis of the water from King's Spring was made by Dr. W. A. Noyes for this paper. He reports on it as follows:

ANALYSIS OF WATER FROM KING'S MINERAL SPRING, NEAR DALLAS, CLARK
COUNTY, INDIANA.

Bases and Acid Radicals.

Bases and Acid Radicals.	Parts per 1,000,000.	Grains per U. S. Gallon.
Calcium (Ca)	456.4	26.624
Magnesium (Mg)	1599.3	93.295
Potassium (K)	76.3	4.451
Sodium (Na)	2177.6	127.030
Chlorine (Cl)	1740.0	101.503
Sulphate (SO_4)	9360.0	546.015
Carbonate (CO_3)	261.6	15.260
Silica (SiO_2)	11.2	.653
Total	15,682.4	914.831

Besides the above there were present traces of alumina, iron,
barium, bromine, and phosphoric acid, and small amounts of manganese, nickel, zinc, strontium, lithium and boric acid.

The elements and acid radicals present may be considered as combined as follows:

	Grains per U. S. Gallon.
Calcium sulphate ($CaSO_4$)	55.937
Calcium carbonate ($CaCO_3$)	25.434
Magnesium sulphate ($MgSO_4$)	466.475
Potassium sulphate (K_2SO_4)	9.935
Sodium chloride (NaCl)	167.264
Sodium sulphate (Na_2SO_4)	189.133
Silica (SiO_2)	0.653
Total	914.831

The analysis shows a water strongly impregnated with Epsom and
Glauber's salts. It is an active cathartic when taken in quantity,
while in smaller doses it is valuable in stomach, liver and intestinal
troubles. It is also advertised as an excellent remedy for scrofulous
diseases and dyspepsia. Miss Jennie King, the owner of the spring,
reports the sale of 700 gallons of the water in 1901, at a price of 10
cents per gallon, which did not include the cost of receptacles.

PAYNE'S MINERAL SPRINGS.

WATER = *Saline-sulphated* (Purgative).

LOCATION.—One mile northwest of Blue Lick Postoffice, Clark
County, on the northwest quarter of Section 251, Clark's Grant.
Three and one-half miles northwest of Memphis, a station on the
Louisville Division of the Pennsylvania Railway, 17 miles north of
Louisville; 93 miles south of Indianapolis.

ORIGIN AND CHARACTER OF THE WATER.—Three springs or seeps, issuing on the slope of a hill which rises 30 to 40 feet above them, have been improved by digging wells 20 feet in depth. In these the water stands eight to ten feet deep and is raised with pumps or with rope and bucket. The springs issue from crevices in the New Providence shale and the water is of the same character as that described from King's Mineral Spring. It has a bitter taste, due to the large quantity of sulphates present, and a temperature, when drawn fresh from the well, of $57\frac{1}{2}°$ F.

An analysis made by Prof. E. T. Cox in 1876, resulted as follows:

ANALYSIS OF MINERAL WATER FROM PAYNE'S SPRINGS, CLARK COUNTY, INDIANA.

	Bases.	*Grains per U. S. Gallon.*
Lime		117.098
Soda		158.632
Potash		50.117
Magnesia		3.149
Alumina		2.916

Acid Radicals.

Chlorine		23.353
Carbonic acid		32.327
Sulphuric acid		334.863
Total		722.455

These constituents are probably combined as follows:

	Grains per U. S. Gallon.
Calcium sulphate ($CaSO_4$)	184.446
Sodium sulphate (Na_2SO_4)	303.008
Potassium sulphate (K_2SO_4)	92.672
Magnesium sulphate ($MgSO_4$)	9.440
Aluminum sulphate ($Al_2(SO_4)_3$)	9.720
Calcium carbonate ($CaCO_3$)	73.471
Sodium chloride ($NaCl$)	49.698
Total	722.455

"The precipated matter which was filtered out contained silica, oxide of iron, lime and alumina. The quantity of water received was not sufficient to admit of the determination of bromine and iodine, but traces were detected.

"This is a strong and valuable saline sulphur water, a small quantity of which will act as cathartic and diuretic."—*Cox.*

In the circular sent out by Parady Payne, the owner, the following claims are made for the water: "It is an excellent purgative tonic. It causes no pain or griping whatever and requires only a small quantity to keep the system in proper condition. It is not unpleasant to drink, emits no odor, will keep any length of time in clean vessels, air-tight or not, there being no loss of virtue by being exposed to the air. It acts on the stomach, liver, kidneys and bowels, imparts clearness and beauty to the complexion, removes pimples from the skin and cleanses the system of all poisons and impurities. It is a good appetizer and materially aids digestion."

Much of this statement is doubtless true not only of the waters of Payne's Springs, but also of those of all others in the county derived from the New Providence shale. They are, however, so strong in cathartic constituents, that they should not be used indiscriminately, but always upon the advice of a physician.

The water from Payne's Springs has been sold many years in Louisville, Jeffersonville, New Albany and Indianapolis. It brings $5.00 per barrel, $3.00 per half barrel or 20 cents per gallon in jugs, f. o. b. at Memphis. A limited number of guests have, in the past, been accommodated at the farm house of Mr. Payne. It is his intention to enlarge his house during the coming season so that he can take care of all who may apply.

INDIANA BLUE LICK SPRING.

WATER = *Saline-sulphated* (Purgative).

LOCATION.—One-half mile west of Blue Lick Postoffice, and three miles northwest of Memphis, Clark County, on Section 250, Clark's Grant. One mile southwest of Payne's Mineral Springs above described.

ORIGIN AND CHARACTER OF THE WATER.—A well sunk to a depth of 11 feet is at the foot of a slope where the water formerly seeped forth from crevices in the shale. In this well the water stands six feet deep and is raised with a rope and bucket. At the residence of the owner, Mr. L. D. Townsend, 30 rods from the well, on the crest of the slope above the latter, cistern water is used for household purposes. It is also used at all other residences in the vicinity, as the bitter mineral water is struck as soon as a well reaches the underlying or New Providence shale. The water of the Townsend well is clear and odorless, has the bitter taste of Epsom and Glauber's salts and a temperature of 58° F. No analysis was available. It possesses, doubtless, the same mineral salts as the Payne and King waters above described and is useful for the same diseases. About 20 barrels per year have been shipped, chiefly to Bedford and Jeffersonville, Ind.

SAMSON KING MINERAL WELL.

WATER = *Saline-sulphated* (Purgative).

LOCATION.—On the northwest quarter of Section 233, Clark's Grant, four miles west of Memphis, on the Louisville Division of the Pennsylvania Railway. Three miles from Wilson's Switch on the C., I. & L. Railway. Postoffice, Blue Lick.

ORIGIN AND CHARACTER OF THE WATER.—The well which formerly produced the Samson King Mineral Water, is situated on top of a hill which rises 40 feet above the valley of Blue Lick Creek. This was the first well or spring in Clark County from which water from the New Providence shale was sold or used to any extent for medicinal purposes. It was dug about 1870 in search of fresh water by Samson King. He passed through five feet of soil, 27 feet of soapstone and 33 feet of "blue rock" (Knobstone). At the depth of 65 feet a fissure was struck in the rock, through which the mineral water entered and filled the well to a depth of 33 feet. An analysis of the water was made by Prof. E. T. Cox, who reported on it as follows:

ANALYSIS OF MINERAL WATER FROM SAMSON KING WELL, CLARK COUNTY, INDIANA.

	Grains per U. S. Gallon.
Calcium sulphate ($CaSO_4$)	59.814
Magnesium sulphate ($MgSO_4$)	357.907
Sodium chloride ($NaCl$)	238.313
Sodium and potassium sulphates	170.265
Total	826.299

Mr. King built a large frame hotel and bath room, advertised freely, and the water had quite a patronage until his death. The place was then transferred to a Mrs. McCabe who carried on the business for some time, selling the water as "Silver King Mineral Water." The well in time partially caved in and no use has been made of the water since 1898.

In 1900 a new spring was discovered about one-eighth of a mile northwest, on the same tract of land, seeping from the side of a slope, 40 feet lower than the surface of the old well. This was dug out to a depth of 12 feet, and in it, in October, 1901, the water was eight feet deep. The output is about ten gallons per hour, of a very clear water, having a temperature of 58° F. The taste is quite bitter and the medicinal virtues are doubtless the same as the waters of the neighboring springs of the same horizon. The new spring is owned by Catherine King, and the water will, in the future, be sold.

* * *

Besides the above, other springs and wells producing a saline water of the same character, have been located in Clark County, on the land of Augustus Reid, Section 27 (1 N., 6 E.); on Sections 4 and 5 (1 S., 6 E.); two miles north of Henryville, on the land of John Stewart, southwest quarter of Section 31 (2 N., 7 E.), and one mile east of the same town on the northeast quarter of Section 241, Clark's Grant. Wherever seeps or springs issue from the New Providence shale, or where wells are sunk to that formation, the chances are that the water will be found heavily charged with the mineral salts mentioned above as occurring in the King, Payne and other waters.

CHARLESTOWN "BLUE LICK SPRING."

WATER = *Saline-sulphuretted* (?).

LOCATION.—One mile northeast of the town of Charlestown, Clark County, on the northwest quarter of Section 97, Clark's Grant. The Louisville Division of the B. & O. S.-W. Railway passes through Charlestown, which is 17 miles northeast of Louisville.

ORIGIN AND CHARACTER OF THE WATER.—The spring issues from the side of a low bluff of Corniferous limestone, and flows into "Lick Run," a small stream a short distance away. The flow, at the time of my visit, in June, 1901, was weak, not over one-half gallon per minute. A white coating of sulphur covered the sides of the rock about the outlet and a distinct but slight odor of hydrogen sulphide was present. The water was clear, cool, and had an agreeable sweetish saline taste, very different from that of the bitter blue lick "sulphated" waters of the northwestern part of the county.

The spring is located in a very pretty woodland, much visited by picnic parties and citizens of the town. It would be an admirable spot for a sanitarium were the supply of water greater. No analysis of the water has ever been made. It is said to be laxative in effect, and is often used by the citizens of Charlestown for skin diseases and rheumatism.

CRAWFORD COUNTY.

WHITE SULPHUR WELL.

WATER = *Saline-sulphuretted.*

LOCATION.—At Sulphur Postoffice, southeast quarter Section 35, (3 S., 1 W.), 12 miles southwest of English, the nearest railway station, on the St. Louis Division of the Southern Railway; eight miles west of Leavenworth and six miles and a half north of Otisco—steamer landings on the Ohio River. A daily stage, carrying mail, express and baggage, runs between English and the well. A livery stable and a stage line are operated in connection with the hotel at the well.

ORIGIN AND CHARACTER OF THE WATER.—The artesian well, from which the water at present flows at the rate of about 10 gallons per minute, is in a wooded grove on the banks of the west fork of the Little Blue River. It was started in search of oil in 1862; but at a depth of 284 feet near the base of the St. Louis limestone a heavy flow of mineral water was struck which stopped farther drilling. According to Professor Collett, the section of the bore above the vein of water was as follows:*

SECTION OF EATON'S WHITE SULPHUR WELL, CRAWFORD COUNTY, INDIANA.

	Ft.
Soil, level of Kaskaskia limestone	21
Chester sandstone and shale	175
Chester and St. Louis limestone with many clay partings	88
Total	284

When the vein of water was reached it "rushed up the well with tremendous force, carrying with it the tools, and put a stop to further boring. An ineffectual attempt was made to test the height to which the well would throw water. A wooden tube, 45 feet long, was placed in the mouth of the bore, and the water flowed over the top, but the hydrostatic pressure was so great that it burst the bottom of the tube, and water was forced through the earth for many feet around."†.

An analysis of the water was made in the laboratory of the State Geological Survey by Dr. G. M. Levette, the chemist of the Department, and published in the report for 1878, p. 515. This showed the mineral ingredients to be as follows:‡

---

*Geological Survey of Indiana, 1878, p. 443.
†Geological Survey of Indiana, 1872, p. 155.
‡In the report cited, the result of analysis was given in grains per imperial gallon. This has been reduced to grains per U. S. gallon.

ANALYSIS OF WHITE SULPHUR WATER, CRAWFORD COUNTY, INDIANA.

Elements and Acid Radicals.	Grains per U. S. Gallon.
Ferrous oxide	1.233
Lime	22.702
Magnesia	19.900
Potash	2.916
Soda	4.748
Sodium	49.305
Sulphuric acid	44.726
Carbon dioxide	41.329
Chlorine	76.089
Total	262.949

The above constituents are probably combined as follows:

	Grains per U. S. Gallon.
Calcium carbonate ($CaCO_3$)	47.498
Magnesium carbonate ($MgCO_3$)	16.793
Calcium sulphate ($CaSO_4$)	11.449
Magnesium sulphate ($MgSO_4$)	43.962
Sodium sulphate (Na_2SO_4)	10.950
Potassium sulphate (K_2SO_4)	5.397
Sodium chloride ($NaCl$)	125.394
Carbonate of iron (Fe_2CO_3)	1.989
Total	263.432

The amount of hydrogen sulphide was not determined by Dr. Levette at the well, but in the samples taken to the laboratory he found 1.96 cubic inches per U. S. gallon. That much more exists is proven by the odor and the bubbles of gas escaping. Part of the gas, however, is undoubtedly carbon dioxide. The analysis shows the water to be saline-sulphuretted in character and to possess valuable medicinal salts. The circulars issued by the company contain numerous testimonials of people who claim to have been highly benefited by its use, especially where taken for stomach diseases, rheumatism, eczema and skin troubles in general.

As it flows from the well the temperature of the water is 58° F. and it is very clear and sparkling. The taste is slightly bitter, due to the sulphates present. The water at present rises about seven feet above the surface in a four-inch closed pipe from which three pipes lead to the bath rooms and bottling works near by. By an arrangement of a wire and pulley the water is taken from the well up to the hotel in a bucket. When this is lowered it fills itself automatically in the stone basin at the base of the outlet pipe in the well.

Besides its use at the hotel and in the bath rooms, large quantities of the water are bottled and shipped, the principal markets being the cities along the "Air-Line" Railway and the Ohio River. A concentrated form produced by boiling 16 gallons down to one, is also bottled and sold under the name "16 to 1 White Sulphur Water."

IMPROVEMENTS.—A three-story hotel and annex has been built on a natural terrace 85 feet above the well. A flight of steps leads down to the well, while a gradual incline skirts the hill, giving an easy path to the infirm and leisurely inclined. The hotel is surrounded by a fine natural grove of beech, oak, walnut and other native forest trees. Wide verandas, swings, music and dancing halls and bowling alleys afford abundant means of recreation. The climb from well to hotel affords also a method of exercise which, while not compulsive, is highly exhilarating. The bath house is located in the valley close to the well and has facilities for hot and cold baths. The hotel is open to guests from April to November. The fresh water used in it is piped by gravity from a spring 1,600 feet distant and located on a hillside 40 feet above the hotel. It is of the purest quality and the supply is abundant even in the driest season. As a place of peaceful quiet, far removed from all nerve-jarring sounds of commerce and travel; surrounded by romantic scenery and pure air, and blessed with an abundance of water, both mineral and pure, the "White Sulphur" resort of Crawford County is highly recommended.

Thirteen miles east of White Sulphur Well, near Great Blue River, the dividing line between Crawford and Harrison counties, is Wyandotte Cave, one of the largest and most beautiful caverns in the United States, furnishing, as it does, at least 12 miles of underground travel if one visits all of its passages. While Wyandotte does not equal Mammoth Cave, Kentucky, in size, it far surpasses it in the grandeur of its scenery. One view alone, that of "Rothrock's Cathedral by Moonlight," is well worthy a journey of hundreds of miles to see. The situation of Wyandotte among the rugged hills which form the breaks of the Ohio River, in a country as yet primitive in character, where game is plentiful, and fishing in the clear waters of Blue River exceptionally good, make it a most inviting spot for a summer's outing.

Around the hotel, situated close to the cave, on a commanding eminence in a natural wooded grove, grow numerous forms of plant life which are strangers to central and northern Indiana, while in the cave dwell many sightless animals whose habits of life are yet unknown; so that the botanist and zoölogist may add to the study of the cavern itself the pursuit of their favorite subjects.

An electric railway could be readily constructed from Corydon, the county seat of Harrison County, 11 miles, to Wyandotte Cave, and from there by way of Leavenworth to White Sulphur Well. Blue River possesses the best undeveloped water power in the State of Indiana, and by the construction of a dam or two it will easily furnish ten times the power necessary for operating the railway and lighting the cave. Stone suitable in every way for building the dams and ballasting the road exists in inexhaustible quantities just where needed. The best of railway ties can be secured at 25 cents apiece, or even less, as thousands are gotten out and floated down Blue River to the Ohio each season.

If thought best, the railway could be constructed along the New Albany and Corydon Pike between New Albany and Corydon. It would thus furnish direct transportation by electric line to the citizens of Louisville, Jeffersonville and New Albany to and from the cave and well. The line, as proposed, would pass, for the most of the way, through a good farming region, and would furnish freight facilities, now lacking, to one of the best fruit raising districts of southern Indiana. A company with the necessary capital, and with men of energy in control, could, without doubt, make of such a road a paying investment. Its construction would make easy of access to the public two of the most worthy and attractive pleasure and health resorts in the United States which are now known only to a few, because of their inaccessibility.

TAR SPRINGS.

WATER = *Alkaline-saline.*

LOCATION.—Three and a half miles northwest of White Sulphur Well, on the southeast quarter of Section 15 (3 S., 1 W.), and seven miles southwest of English, the nearest railway station, on the St. Louis Division of the Southern Railway.

ORIGIN AND CHARACTER OF THE WATER.—These springs were not visited, but I was reliably informed that the conditions are practically the same as in 1878, when Professor Collett wrote of them as follows: "Two weak springs have outlets from beneath the Kaskaskia limestone, just below a bed of Conglomerate, in a deep, wild valley. The west spring discharges with its waters coal tar and carburetted hydrogen; the outlet is in a basin trough, built up on the rocks, of earth cemented with the deposited asphaltum. The east spring, thirteen feet distant from the last, discharges water and petroleum, with a small quantity of carburetted hydrogen gas. Both are strong flowing fountains during rainy weather, but are weak during dry seasons.

"Some instinct of nature, or reason, attracts all domestic animals to these springs; in malarial seasons hogs and cattle will break from enclosures and go miles to obtain the water, while pure spring and brook water is plentiful nearer by. There is no saline taste perceptible, but we may infer that there is some remedial effect experienced by the animals after drinking it. I am informed by Mr. T. Roberson that domestic animals not only drink the water greedily, but when foot and mouth diseases are prevalent they manifest a desire to bathe the diseased parts in the oily fluid. It is probable that this spring and other "oil seeps" induced the boring of the six wells which were put down during the "oil fever" of 1862-66.*"

- The analysis of the water, made by Dr. Levette and published on page 516 of the report cited, showed the mineral ingredients to be as follows:

ANALYSIS OF WATER FROM THE "TAR SPRING," CRAWFORD COUNTY, INDIANA.

Elements and Acid Radicals.	Grains per U. S. Gallon.
Ferric oxide	2.332
Lime	8.397
Magnesia	3.649
Potash	0.916
Soda	1.541
Sulphuric acid	8.765
Carbonic acid	16.053
Total	41.653

The above constituents are probably combined as follows:

	Grains.
Calcium carbonate (CaCO₃)	21.596
Magnesium carbonate (MgCO₃)	2.078
Magnesium sulphate (MgSO₄)	8.995
Sodium sulphate (Na₂SO₄)	3.529
Potassium sulphate (K₂SO₄)	1.696
Carbonate of iron (FeCO₃)	3.758
Total	41.652

"This water has a slight odor of petroleum, with a few globules of oily matter floating on the surface. It contained no hydro-sulphuric acid or chlorine."

---

*Geological Survey of Indiana, 1878, p. 445.

HAZLEWOOD SULPHUR WELL.

WATER = *Saline-sulphuretted.*

LOCATION.—On the land of Dr. George R. Hazlewood, along the west bank of Little Blue River, south half of section 13 (2 S., 1 W.), one-half mile north of the station of the St. Louis Division of the Southern Railway, at English.

ORIGIN AND CHARACTER OF THE WATER.—The water at present flows from an artesian boring 32 feet deep, at the rate of about two gallons per minute. Prior to 1890 it issued from several springs in a basin which has been excavated and cemented close to the bank of the creek. In the first settlement of the country these springs were known as "Elk Springs" or "Elk Lick," as elk and other wild beasts used to frequent the place, probably for the salt which the water held in solution, and that which was left in the surrounding soil by evaporation. A large hotel and sanitarium, which was run under the name of the "Hartford Sulphur Spring," was erected in 1885, but burned in 1889. The water at that time had a wide reputation and many patients and visitors patronized the resort. When the bore was sunk 10 rods northwest of the spring, so as to have the water nearer the dwelling erected on the site of the hotel, the flow of the spring grew less and finally ceased.

Dr. Levette, in 1878, analyzed the water, finding its mineral ingredients to be as follows:

ANALYSIS OF WATER FROM HAZLEWOOD SULPHUR WELL, CRAWFORD COUNTY, INDIANA.

Elements and Acid Radicals.	*Grains per U. S. Gallon.*
Ferric oxide	1.166
Lime	10.413
Magnesia	7.064
Potash	0.708
Soda	3.515
Sodium	23.864
Sulphuric acid	16.786
Carbonic acid	19.776
Chlorine	36.827
Total	120.119

*Geological Survey of Indiana, 1878, p. 518.

PLATE II.

ARTESIAN MINERAL WELL IN ENGLISH PARK, ENGLISH,
CRAWFORD COUNTY, INDIANA.

The above constituents are probably combined as follows:

	Grains.
Calcium carbonate ($CaCO_3$)	20.568
Magnesium carbonate ($MgCO_3$)	9.459
Calcium sulphate ($CaSO_4$)	5.866
Magnesium sulphate ($MgSO_4$)	12,296
Sodium sulphate (Na_2SO_4)	8.051
Potassium sulphate (K_2SO_4)	1.310
Sodium chloride ($NaCl$)	60.691
Total	120.119

In August, 1901, the water flowed from a pipe three feet above the ground. Both odor and taste of hydrogen sulphide were distinct, but not strong. The temperature was 65° F. The characteristic white sulphur deposit lined the receiving basin and coated the sides of the rill bearing away the overflow. Dr. Hazlewood, the owner, claims the water to be anti-acid and diuretic rather than purgative; and stated that when the sanitarium was in operation it was the custom to secretly sink a bag of Epsom salts in one of the springs during the night in order to increase the purgative properties of the water. At present only local use is made of the water, and that has decreased largely since the flowing wells have been developed in English Park.

ENGLISH ARTESIAN WELLS.

WATER = *Saline-sulphuretted* (?).

LOCATION.—In a public park four squares northwest of the court house and three squares west of the railway station at English, the county seat, a town of 800 inhabitants, located on the St. Louis Division of the Southern Railway ("Air Line"), 46 miles northwest of Louisville and 228 miles east of St. Louis.

ORIGIN AND CHARACTER OF THE WATER.—These wells, two in number, were sunk in 1899 to depths of 817 and 860 feet, respectively, in search of oil or gas. They lacked 1,000 feet or more, however, of reaching the Trenton limestone, the main oil and gas horizon of the State. The wells are 100 yards apart in English Park, a rather low tract of land lying in the angle between the junction of Little Blue River and Camp Creek, and along the north side of the "Air-Line" Railway.

The mineral water in both was struck at a depth of approximately 700 feet. A pure water was struck at a higher level and cased off, but is said to now mingle with the mineral water before reaching the surface, thereby weakening the latter. Only the northernmost of the two wells at present flows, though the water in the other, which was the first drilled, stands eight inches above the surface in the protruding iron casing, and would flow were the casing removed. When the flow of one is stopped the other immediately begins, and the pipes and levels could be so arranged as to cause a good flow from each. In August, 1901, the water was rushing forth from the drive-pipe of the flowing well, three feet above the surface, at the rate of 15 or more gallons per minute. It was clear and sparkling; had a temperature of 56° F.; a slightly bitter taste and a weak odor of hydrogen sulphide. This gas was, however, sufficient in quantity to coat with a deposit of sulphur the nearby objects. No analysis of the water was available. It is much used locally in bilious diseases, and is said to be a strong purgative.

DAVIESS COUNTY.

CABLE & CO., No. 4 MINERAL WELL.

WATER = *Saline-sulphated.*

LOCATION.—About one and one-half miles south of Washington, the county seat, a city of 9,000 population, situated on the B. & O. S.-W. Railway, 173 miles west of Cincinnati and 168 miles east of St. Louis; and on the E. & I. Railway, 58 miles north of Evansville, and 80 miles southeast of Terre Haute.

ORIGIN AND CHARACTER OF THE WATER.—This well was drilled 800 feet deep in search of coal. It is on the southwest quarter of Section 3 (2 N., 7 W.), near the No. 4 Mine of Cable & Co. At the bottom of the well, in a grayish shale, a strong vein of mineral water was encountered, which flowed four feet above the surface for some years. The well was finally plugged, as the water ran into the mine in too great quantity. The plug can, however, be removed at any time, and the water be rendered once more available.

An analysis made for the owners by Werner & Simonson, of Cincinnati, showed the presence of the following mineral salts:

ANALYSIS OF WATER FROM CABLE & CO.'S NO. 4 WELL, WASHINGTON, INDIANA.

	Grains per U. S. Gallon.
Calcium sulphate ($CaSO_4$)	75.712
Calcium carbonate ($CaCO_3$)	9.256
Magnesium chloride ($MgCl_2$)	88.480
Magnesium bromide ($MgBr_2$)	0.605
Potassium sulphate (K_2SO_4)	7.168
Sodium sulphate (Na_2SO_4)	488.088
Sodium chloride ($NaCl$)	1014.336
Total	1683.645

A small quantity of lithium was found. The water was wholly free from nitrogenous organic matter.

When last seen by the writer, in 1895, the flow was about 15 gallons per minute. The water was without odor, but was quite salty in taste. Large quantities were being carried away daily in jugs and kegs by the citizens of Washington and vicinity. It was claimed to be especially valuable in skin and kidney diseases and for rheumatism.

DEARBORN COUNTY.

AURORA ARTESIAN WELL.

WATER = Saline-sulphuretted.

LOCATION.—In the western portion of Aurora, a city of 3,700 inhabitants, located on the Ohio River, 26 miles below Cincinnati. Accessible by steamers on the Ohio; by the B. & O. S.-W. and Big Four railways, and by the Cincinnati, Lawrenceburg and Aurora Electric Railway.

ORIGIN AND CHARACTER OF THE WATER.—The artesian well at Aurora is on the bank of South Hogan Creek, within a few rods of the station of the B. & O. S.-W. Railway. It was sunk about 1890 in search of natural gas, to a depth of 366 feet; the water being found about 10 feet below the top of the Trenton limestone. In July, 1901, the water was flowing from a two-inch pipe, four feet above the ground, at the rate of about seven gallons per minute.

A partial analysis was made a number of years ago by Dr. W. Dickore, of Cincinnati, who reported on it as follows:

ANALYSIS OF AURORA ARTESIAN WATER.

Total solids, 564.16 grains to the U. S. gallon. These are present in the following forms:
Sodium chloride (three-quarters of the whole amount).
Magnesium sulphate or chloride.
Calcium carbonate and sulphate.
Potassium sulphate or chloride.
Iron carbonate.
Silicic acid (trace).
Lithia (trace).
Magnesium bromide (trace).
Magnesium iodide (trace).
The free gases present are sulphuretted hydrogen and carbonic acid gas.

The water is known locally as "Blue Lick" and has an agreeable sweetish-saline taste. The amount of hydrogen sulphide present is not great, but sufficient to give its distinctive odor to the air a rod or two away from the well. It is said that the water will hold its gas for several days without becoming "flat." It is recommended by the physicians of Aurora for catarrh and skin diseases, especially eczema and ivy poisoning. It is also said to be very helpful in recovering from the effects of intoxication, and one mud-covered disciple of Bacchus whom I found at 5 o'clock in the morning quaffing long and deep of the water, assured me that "it destroys all feeling of sickness at stomach and headache. One can drink any amount of it after being on a drunk and it will help him every time." Many citizens carry it home in jugs for use as a mild laxative and diuretic. Quantities are also shipped, though no person, as far as could be learned, controls this shipment. The well is owned by a local stock company and the water is free to all users. It offers excellent advantages to a party with capital who desires to erect a sanitarium and bath house, as there is no similar water so readily accessible in southeastern Indiana.

CHEEK'S SPRING.

WATER = *Saline-sulphuretted* (?).

LOCATION.—In the city of Aurora, one-third of a mile north of the artesian well above described.

ORIGIN AND CHARACTER OF THE WATER.—The spring issues from the base of a low bluff a few rods north of the B. & O. S.-W. Railway track. The flow is small, probably not over 20 gallons per hour, into a pond lying between the railway track and the spring.

No analysis was available. The water has a bitter taste, indicating the presence of sulphates of magnesia and soda. It is said to smell strongly of sulphuretted hydrogen at times, and the water of cisterns near by has been so affected by the same gas as to be useless. Before the drilling of the artesian well the water of Cheek's Spring was much used locally for rheumatism, and as a purgative and diuretic.

DUBOIS COUNTY.

JASPER ARTESIAN WELL.

WATER = *Saline-sulphuretted* (?).

LOCATION.—One-third of a mile southeast of the court house at Jasper, the county seat, a town of 2,000 inhabitants, on the St. Louis Division of the Southern Railway, 82 miles west of Louisville and 206 miles east of St. Louis.

ORIGIN AND CHARACTER OF THE WATER.—The artesian well is located on a terrace just west of the Patoka River, near the east line of Section 35 (1 S., 5 W.). It was sunk in 1889, in search of oil or gas, to a depth of 1,009 feet, but lacked several hundred feet of reaching Trenton limestone. At 720 feet the drill pierced a soft blue limestone, from which issued a water strongly charged with hydrogen sulphide. This was so offensive to the nostrils of the citizens that the well was filled up to 713 feet, at which depth the present issuing mineral water had been found.

No analysis of the water was available. In September, 1901, it was flowing at the rate of four gallons per minute. The temperature at the end of the discharge pipe, 40 feet from the well, was 62° F. The water had an agreeable, slightly saline taste. The odor of hydrogen sulphide was present, but weak. Enough gas, probably carburetted hydrogen, was issuing from the pipe to burn when ignited, with a small but constant flame. It is said that at times for a few days the water becomes murky, much more bitter, and strongly impregnated with hydrogen sulphide, after which it clears up and remains clear for several weeks. It may be that this change is caused by an accumulation of gas forcing some of the stronger mineral water up from the lower vein and causing a mixture of the two waters. The water is used by many of the citizens of Jasper as a laxative and diuretic. In appearance and properties, as far as could be judged without an analysis, it is fully equal to many similar waters which are used in sanitariums with excellent curative results.

TOUSSAINT DUBOIS SPRING.

WATER = Neutral.

LOCATION.—On the farm of Fritz Mann, northeast quarter Section 3 (1 S., 5 W.), Boone Township, five miles northwest of Jasper.

ORIGIN AND CHARACTER OF THE WATER.—This spring bubbles up in an artesian flow about 50 feet from Mill Creek. According to Prof. Geo. R. Wilson "it flows a strong stream and its waters are noted for their purity. An analysis of its waters by Dr. John Hurty, of Indianapolis, shows its ingredients to be as follows: Thirty-two grains of chalk (carbonate of lime) and the slightest trace of iron in one gallon."[*]

[*] "History and Art Souvenir of Dubois County," 1896, p. 9.

ELKHART COUNTY.

LAMBERT MINERAL WELL.

WATER = *Saline-carbonated.*

LOCATION.—In the south part of the city of Elkhart, one-half mile from the center, and about the same distance from the southern limits. Elkhart is a city of 16,000 population, located 101 miles east of Chicago on the Lake Shore and Michigan Southern Railway, and 157 miles north of Indianapolis, on the Michigan Division of the Big Four Railway. The Indiana Electric Railway, operating between South Bend and Goshen, also runs its cars within three blocks of the well.

ORIGIN AND CHARACTER OF THE WATER.—The well which produces the water in question was started some years ago in search of oil or gas. At a depth of 290 feet a strong vein of mineral water was found, which arose to within 14 feet of the surface.

An analysis of the water by Dr. W. A. Noyes, of Terre Haute, resulted as follows:

ANALYSIS OF LAMBERT MINERAL WATER, ELKHART, INDIANA.

Elements and Acid Radicals.	Parts to 1,000,000.
Calcium	380.0
Magnesium	132.7
Sodium	4660.0
Potassium	72.4
Chlorine	8137.0
Carbon dioxide	127.0
Silica	7.4
Alumina	.8
Iron	.3
Total	13517.6

The substances in the water may be considered as combined essentially as follows:

	Grains per U. S. Gallon.
Calcium chloride ($CaCl_2$)	54.520
Calcium carbonate ($CaCO_3$)	6.300
Magnesium chloride ($MgCl_2$)	30.643
Sodium chloride (NaCl)	686.077
Potassium chloride (KCl)	8.050
Silica (SiO_2)	.432
Alumina (Al_2O_3)	.047
Ferrous carbonate ($FeCo_3$)	.035
Total	786.104

Carbon dioxide, free and as bi-carbonate—10,088 cu. in. per gallon.

Besides the above, a trace each of strontium chloride, lithium chloride, sodium bromide and sodium borate were present. The water is remarkable for the absence of sulphates.

This is a water strongly impregnated with common salt, and when pumped has a temperature of 54° F. It is very clear, and sparkles with the carbonic acid gas which it holds in solution. It is without odor and has a salty but not disagreeable taste. The minerals present are held in such chemical affinity that they do not precipitate readily. The water can thus be shipped or carried a distance and still retain its natural properties. As yet it has had only a local use, being furnished free to all who apply.

The well is located on high and spacious grounds. The buildings already in use can be readily converted into a sanitarium, and, as no other similar water is known to occur in northern Indiana, an excellent location for a medical sanitarium is presented.

FLOYD COUNTY.

BRIGGS MINERAL SPRING.

WATER = *Saline-sulphated.*

LOCATION.—One mile northwest of the court house at New Albany, the county seat, a city of 21,000 population; situated on the Ohio River, opposite Louisville, Kentucky. Accessible by steamer on the Ohio and by the C., I. & L. (Monon), Pennsylvania, Big Four, and the St. Louis Division of the Southern railways; also by electric lines from Louisville.

ORIGIN AND CHARACTER OF THE WATER.—The Briggs Mineral Spring issues from the base of a wooded bluff which slopes up to a height of 75 or more feet, just outside the city limits. This bluff is composed, for the most part, of New Providence shale, a fine grained, greenish-gray material, containing many nodules and bands of siderite or iron carbonate. This shale is the source of the water of all the mineral springs of Clark County, described on a preceding page. The lower slope of the bluff in the immediate vicinity of the Briggs Spring has been much eroded and cut up into gullies, and the weathered shale is in many places wholly devoid of vegetation. On account of disuse, the visible flow of water from the spring is at present small, being not over 12 gallons per hour.

An analysis of the water by Prof. J. F. Elsom, made in 1883, when it was extensively used, showed its mineral ingredients to be as follows:

4—Geol.

ANALYSIS OF WATER FROM BRIGGS SPRING, FLOYD COUNTY, INDIANA.

	Grains per U. S. Gallon.
Magnesium carbonate (MgCO₃)	2.936
Calcium carbonate (CaCO₃)	29.728
Sodium chloride (NaCl)	18.536
Potassium sulphate (K₂SO₄)	4.072
Magnesium sulphate (MgSO₄)	263.280
Ferrous carbonate (FeCO₃)	.1416
Calcium sulphate (CaSO₄)	31.896
Total	350.5896

When visited, in September, 1901, the temperature of the water was 57° F. The taste is quite bitter, due to the large percentage of sulphates present. For a number of years the water was bottled and sold quite extensively in Louisville and New Albany. It was also delivered to customers in New Albany at 15 cents a gallon. The ownership changed hands and the sale was gradually abandoned. The water contains the same constituents as the Clark County mineral waters and is in every way as valuable as they.

FOUNTAIN COUNTY.

LODI ARTESIAN WELL.

WATER = *Saline-sulphuretted.*

LOCATION.—On the east bank of the old Wabash and Erie Canal, one mile northwest of Silverwood, a station on the T., St. L. & W. (Clover Leaf) Railway, 191 miles east of St. Louis and 263 miles southwest of Toledo, Ohio. From Cayuga, the crossing of the "Clover Leaf" and C. & E. I. railways, the well is distant three and a half miles east, the Wabash River intervening. The distance by rail to Cayuga from Terre Haute is 37 miles; from Chicago 141 miles.

ORIGIN AND CHARACTER OF THE WATER.—This well, which furnishes one of the best, if not the best, undeveloped sites for a mineral water sanitarium in the State, was drilled in 1865 to a depth of 1,155 feet in search of oil. It is located near the center of the northern half of Section 35 (18 N., 9 W.), on a farm belonging to Mrs. Mary F. Safely, of Rockville, Ind. Several veins of salt water were struck in the bore and at 1,057 feet, in a magnesian limestone, a strong vein of mineral water was developed, which burst forth with great violence.

An analysis of the water was made, a year or two after it was struck, by Dr. J. C. Pohle, of New York City, and another in 1884 by Dr. C. F. Chandler, of the same city. These analyses are both given herewith:

ANALYSES OF WATER FROM THE LODI ARTESIAN WELL.

	POHLE.	CHANDLER.
	Grains per U. S. Gallon.	
Sodium chloride (NaCl)	502.464	523.058
Calcium chloride (CaCl₂)	47.928	21.774
Magnesium chloride (MgCl₂)	53.540	57.895
Calcium sulphate (CaSo₄)	55.553	40.240
Potassium sulphate (K₂SO₄)	.804	13.598
Magnesium sulphate (MgSO₄)	3.260	.....
Sodium sulphate (Na₂SO₄)	2.135	1.412
Calcium bi-carbonate (CaH₂(CO₃)₂)	2.904	53.593
Magnesium bi-carbonate (MgH₂(CO₃)₂)	1.104	.....
Magnesium bromide	.880	.....
Sodium bromide	.....	1.409
Silicic acid (H₄SiO₄)	.520	.472
Calcium phosphate (Ca₃PO₄)	1.200	.065
Lithium chloride (LiCl)	.....	.749
Totals	672.292	714.265
Hydrogen sulphide, cu. in. per gal	7.94	4.64

It will be noted that the two analyses differ materially in the amounts of calcium chloride, potassium sulphate and calcium bi-carbonate present, and to a less extent in the amounts of a number of the other salts. The comparison could have been much more exact if the percentage of each of the elements and acid radicals present had been shown in each instance, but these were not furnished by the chemists.

It is said that the flow has decreased little, if any, in the 37 years since the well was drilled. In August, 1901, the water was bubbling with great force over the top of a four-inch wooden pipe eight feet above the surface, the estimated output being 30,000 barrels per day. Iron pipes are eaten through in a year or two, so are not used. The temperature of the water as it left the well was 69° F. The odor of hydrogen sulphide was very strong, and free sulphur from this gas had coated a yellowish white all objects within 20 feet of the well. The taste of the water is a bitter-saline, somewhat disagreeable at first, but relished after a time. According to Dr. George T. Deverter, of Silverwood, it is slightly laxative and a most excellent remedy for all skin troubles, such as eczema, eruptions due to heat, and for kidney troubles. At present it is much used locally, and to some extent is shipped, bringing $4.00 per barrel on board the cars at Silverwood, or 50 cents per gallon in jugs.

IMPROVEMENTS.—A large residence and hotel, erected about 1880 by the former owner, Mr. J. J. Safely, was burned a few years later and has not been rebuilt. A bath house, with cement-lined pool. 60x20 feet, and averaging four and a half feet in depth, is connected with the well, and is open during the summer months. There are no facilities for heating the water. A fine grove of timber lies adjacent to the well and bath house, and is much frequented by campers and picnic parties during the warm season. Taking into consideration the quality and quantity of the water, the railway facilities and the natural surroundings, this well offers a most excellent site for parties who wish to erect a large sanitarium and resort for invalids.

ATTICA ARTESIAN WELL.

WATER = *Saline-sulphuretted.*

LOCATION.—Near the southern limits of Attica, a city of 3,100 population, situated on the Wabash River in the northern portion of the county. The Wabash Railway and the Brazil division of the C. & E. I. Railway cross in the city, thus furnishing easy transportation in all directions. The distance from Chicago is 118 miles; from Indianapolis, via the Big Four to Covington, 87 miles; from St. Louis, 211 miles; from Lafayette, 21 miles.

ORIGIN AND CHARACTER OF THE WATER.—The mineral water at Attica does not come from a spring, as commonly advertised, but from an artesian well, which was sunk in 1889 to a depth of 865 feet. A strong flow of saline-sulphur water was struck at a depth of 600 feet, which has since continued unabated.

An analysis of the water by Prof. H. A. Huston, of Purdue University, proved the presence of the following ingredients:

ANALYSIS OF WATER FROM ATTICA ARTESIAN WELL.

	Grains per U. S. Gallon.
Calcium sulphate ($CaSO_4$)	4.10
Sodium chloride ($NaCl$)	338.82
Potassium chloride (KCl)	trace
Lithium chloride ($LiCl$)	1.16
Magnesium chloride ($MgCl_2$)	14.72
Calcium chloride ($CaCl_2$)	10.13
Calcium carbonate ($CaCO_3$)	21.65
Alumina and iron oxide ($Al_2O_3 \& Fe_2O_3$)	.08
Total	390.66

The flow of water is said to be about 320 gallons per minute. It has an agreeable saline taste, a temperature of 55° F., and a distinct odor of hydrogen sulphide.

IMPROVEMENTS.—The "Lithia Springs Hotel," a large two-story building with accommodations for 80 guests, equipped with modern improvements, and with excellent facilities for giving mineral and Turkish baths, was erected at the site of the well in 1898. Mud baths, for persons afflicted with rheumatism or skin diseases, are also given if desired. The grounds about the hotel are spacious, and it promises to grow in popularity as a resort as the water becomes better known.

WALLACE MINERAL SPRING.

WATER = *Chalybeate.*

LOCATION.—One-fourth of a mile west of Wallace, a village situated in Section 19 (18 N., 6 W.), in the southwest corner of the county. The nearest railway station is Yeddo, seven miles northwest on the Brazil Division of the C. & E. I. Railway.

ORIGIN AND CHARACTER OF THE WATER.—This is one of the strongest flowing chalybeate springs in western Indiana. It issues from a bank of glacial gravel on the roadside, and is in part piped to a watering trough, where it has an extensive local usage by both man and beast. The flow varies slightly with the season, and is between 2,000 and 3,000 gallons per hour. The water contains quite a percentage of iron salts, probably the carbonate, as is shown by the reddish-brown deposit of iron oxide on the watering trough and about the orifice of the spring. No analysis has been made.

There are a number of similar but smaller springs south along Sugar Mill Creek, and one, heavily charged with iron and free carbon dioxide gas, is located three-quarters of a mile west of Wallace. It bubbles up in the bed of a small stream in the middle of the road.

FULTON COUNTY.

FEECE'S MINERAL WELL.

WATER = *Chalybeate.*

LOCATION.—On the southeast quarter Section 24 (30 N., 3 E.), four miles southeast of Rochester, the county seat, a town of 3,500 population, situated on the L. E. & W. and Chicago and Erie Railways, 101 miles southeast of Chicago; 98 miles north of Indianapolis.

ORIGIN AND CHARACTER OF THE WATER.—A well 30 feet deep, sunk in drift (clay and gravel), developed a vein of chalybeate water which rose to within 12 feet of the surface. A trench was dug and an inch pipe put down, which conveys the water 60 or more feet to the side of a bluff, where it emerges as a flowing stream. This passes through a small building, in which a boiler and engine, now out of repair, was used to heat the water. The output from the well is about five gallons per minute. No analysis was available, but the taste and appearance suggest the presence of iron and calcium carbonates and calcium sulphate.

IMPROVEMENTS.—For some years this water had a local reputation. A small bath house and hotel was erected, and the place had, from time to time, a number of guests. The patronage was not sufficient to pay expenses, and for several years no use has been made of the water or buildings.

GIBSON COUNTY.

McCULLOUGH'S SPRING.

WATER = *Alkaline-saline-chalybeate.*

LOCATION.—On the land of D. C. McCullough, a mile and a quarter south of Oakland City, a town of 2,000 inhabitants; situated at the crossing of the E. & I. and Southern Railways, 99 miles west of Louisville, 175 miles east of St. Louis and 28 miles northeast of Evansville.

ORIGIN AND CHARACTER OF THE WATER.—This spring issues by the roadside from the base of a knoll, which rises 15 feet above the lower land, along which the overflow escapes. The surface of the knoll is of the yellow silty soil peculiar to the county. At the bottom of the spring a stiff blue clay occurs, which is probably a decomposed shale from which the water derives its iron and sulphates. A well-like receptacle for the spring water has been dug and walled up with brick. In this the water stands eight feet deep. An open well-house has been erected over the spring, and a large tile put in above the brick wall. Several springs of similar water, though flowing a smaller quantity, exude along the same bank a few rods to the west. No one of these has been improved.

According to the owner, an analysis of the water was made in 1880 or 1883, by a chemist in Indianapolis, whose name has been forgotten. This resulted as follows:

ANALYSIS OF WATER FROM M'CULLOUGH'S SPRING, OAKLAND CITY, INDIANA.

Grains per U. S. Gallon.

Calcium carbonate (CaCO₃).............................. 36.339

Ferrous carbonate (FeCO₄)............................. 57.920

Ferric sulphate (Fe₂(SO₄)₃)............................ 96.226

Magnesium sulphate (MgSO₄).......................... 87.355

Aluminum sulphate (Al₂(SO₄)₃)........................ 36.407

Sodium chloride (NaCl)................................ 1.784

Potassium chloride (KCl).............................. trace

Total 316.031

The analysis shows an alum-copperas water of excellent quality. It is clear, has a temperature of 65° F. and a very bitter taste. It has been much used locally, and is said to have excellent results in stomach and kidney troubles and malaria, and especially for chronic diarrhea. It is a decided purgative if taken in quantity. The owner ships it to whoever applies, at 25 cents a gallon, but the demand, as yet, is not large.

OWENSVILLE ARTESIAN WELL.

WATER = *Chalybeate.*

LOCATION.—On the land of Warrick Smith, northwest of the public square and about 200 yards from the corporate limits of Owensville, a town of 1,100 population, situated in the southwestern part of Gibson County, on the Mt. Vernon Branch of the E. & T. H. Railway, 30 miles north of Mt. Vernon and 13 miles southwest of Princeton.

ORIGIN AND CHARACTER OF THE WATER.—This well is a prospect bore put down for coal on the southeast quarter Section 1 (3 N., 12 W.), in 1872 to a depth of 217 feet. The water was struck in a bed of fire-clay and gray shale at the bottom of the well. It has been flowing steadily since. The water has a distinct taste of iron, but is said to contain no sulphur. No analysis has been made. It is used extensively by the citizens of Owensville for drinking purposes. It acts as a laxative when used freely.

GREENE COUNTY.

WORTHINGTON ARTESIAN WELL.

WATER = Saline-sulphuretted.

LOCATION.—In the south part of Worthington, a town of 1,500 inhabitants, located one-half mile southwest of the junction of Eel River and the west fork of White River, at the crossing of the I. & V. and E. & I. Railways. Distance from Indianapolis, 71 miles; from Vincennes, 46 miles; from Evansville, 98 miles; from Terre Haute, 40 miles.

ORIGIN AND CHARACTER OF THE WATER.—This well was drilled for oil or gas in 1890 to a depth of 1,670 feet. At 1,430 feet, in a limestone, probably the Niagara, a strong flow of mineral water was developed. A test showed that this water would rise 65 feet above the surface in a two-inch pipe. It is piped to a public fountain in the center of town, one-third of a mile north of the well.

An incomplete analysis only was available. It was made by Albert H. Prescott, of the University of Michigan, who reported the presence of the following:

ANALYSIS OF WATER FROM WORTHINGTON ARTESIAN WELL.

Hydro-sulphuric acid sulphides.
Chlorides.
Sulphates (in traces).
Bromides (in traces).
Magnesium salts.
Calcium salts.
Sodium salts.
Potassium salts (in traces).

These constituents are chemically united, chiefly as follows:

Sodium sulphide (Na_2S).
Calcium sulphide (CaS).
Magnesium chloride ($MgCl_2$).
Calcium chloride ($CaCl_2$).
Potassium bromide (KBr)
The total quantity of solids is 252 grains per U. S. gallon.

In September, 1901, the flow at the fountain was probably 1,200 gallons per hour. At the well, where but a small escape pipe was open, the temperature was 71° F. From this pipe gas enough was issuing with the water to burn steadily with a flame six inches high when ignited. The odor of hydrogen sulphide was strong, and the escaping gas was probably a mixture of this and carburetted hydrogen. The water was very clear at the well, but at the fountain was somewhat turbid. The taste is slightly bitter and saline, but less so than many other sulphuretted waters. The citizens partake free-ly of it at the fountain. As a remedial agent it is used quite exten-sively for skin diseases and as a diuretic.

The locality about Worthington, especially along the river, is picturesque. Excellent facilities for boating and fishing are pres-ent. A sanitarium and resort could, without doubt, be established which would prove successful under the proper management.

HANCOCK COUNTY.

HALSALL SPRING.

WATER = *Alkaline.*

LOCATION.—On the farm of Maggie L. Halsall, east half of the southeast quarter of Section 12 (16 N., 6 E.), three miles northwest of Greenfield, the county seat, and one and a half miles from Max-well, a station on the Peoria Division of the Big Four Railway, 22 miles east of Indianapolis.

ORIGIN AND CHARACTER OF THE WATER.—A strong flowing spring wells up through the drift on a comparatively level plain. The out-put is 10 gallons per minute of a remarkably clear water, sparkling with numerous bubbles of carbonic acid gas. A large quantity of travertine or calcareous tufa has been deposited by this spring about its mouth and along the rill bearing away the overflow. This is formed of calcium carbonate, which the waters of the spring have dissolved while percolating through beds of gravel and other drift material in the vicinity. As soon as the water charged with this calcium carbonate reaches the surface, the gaseous carbon dioxide is liberated and the calcium carbonate deposited as calcareous tufa. No analysis of the water of this spring has been made.

SPRING LAKE PARK MINERAL WELL.

WATER = *Alkaline-chalybeate.*

LOCATION.—In Spring Lake Park, a tract of 35 acres of wood-land, located 17 miles east of Indianapolis, on the line of the Indi-anapolis & Greenfield Rapid Transit Company, the cars of which run into the park. One-half mile southwest from Philadelphia, a station on the Columbus & Indianapolis Division of the Pennsyl-vania Railway.

ORIGIN AND CHARACTER OF THE WATER.—A well, 17 feet in depth, is situated on a ridge eight feet above the level of a large pond. The

bottom of the well is in a bed of gravel, and yields a large supply
of water, which is raised by a pump. It is clear and odorless, but
tastes strongly of iron oxide. An analysis by T. W. Smith, of Indianapolis, showed the mineral ingredients to be as follows:

ANALYSIS OF WATER FROM SPRING LAKE PARK, HANCOCK COUNTY, INDIANA.

Grains per U. S. Gallon.

Silica (SiO₂)... 0.64
Calcium sulphate (CaSO₄)............................... 1.75
Calcium carbonate (CaCO₃)............................. 0.40
Magnesium carbonate (MgCO₃).......................12.42
Sodium chloride (NaCl)................................. 1.00
Ferrous oxide (FeO)...................................16.27

Total solids...32.48

The analysis shows a water strongly chalybeate in character, and
therefore useful in anemic conditions. It is used extensively by
visitors to the park, of which there are many during the summer
months. The lake in the park is fed by a number of natural springs,
whose waters are also of a chalybeate nature.

HARRISON COUNTY.

CORYDON SULPHUR WELL.

WATER = *Saline-sulphuretted.*

LOCATION.—One and a fourth miles east of Corydon, by the side
of the New Albany and Corydon Turnpike. Corydon, the first capital of Indiana and the present county seat of Harrison County, is
situated in one of the most picturesque regions of southern Indiana.
It is a town of 1,650 population, located on the Louisville, New
Albany & Corydon Railway, 31 miles west of Louisville.

ORIGIN AND CHARACTER OF THE WATER.—In 1871 sulphur water
was found oozing out of the bank at the site of the present well on
the north side of Little Indian Creek. The owner, Mr. Amos Zenor,
began investigations, and finally dug a well 28 feet in depth to a
thick stratum of St. Louis limestone, through a crevice of which
the water welled up in a strong flow. The well was walled with
brick, and the water rose within five feet of the top and then found
its way into the nearby creek.

An incomplete analysis by Dr. T. E. Jenkins, of Louisville, showed the presence of the following salts:

ANALYSIS OF WATER FROM CORYDON SULPHUR WELL.

Sodium bi-carbonate (NaHCO$_3$).
Magnesium bi-carbonate (MgH$_2$(CO$_3$)$_2$).
Sodium sulphate (Na$_2$SO$_4$).
Magnesium sulphate (MgSO$_4$).
Calcium sulphate (CaSO$_4$).
Sodium chloride (NaCl).
Magnesium chloride (MgCl$_2$).
Calcium chloride (CaCl$_2$).
Silica (SiO$_2$).
Total solids in one U. S. gallon, 450.88.
Gases in solution, carbonic acid and hydrogen sulphide.

The underbrush and fallen timber about the well was cleared up a number of years ago, leaving a beautiful grove of oak, cedar, beech, buckeye, butternut, sycamore, mulberry, black willow and other natural forest trees. This wooded tract of 11 acres still exists in all its pristine beauty, furnishing a natural park far surpassing that found about any other mineral well or spring of Indiana, French Lick excepted. At the time of my visit, in October, 1901, I walked in early morn from the center of Corydon, nestled among her hills and shaded by rows of great spreading elms, out to the sulphur well, and was forcibly impressed by the quiet beauty of the place. The old stone State House and the "legislative elm;" Indian Creek rippling gently over her rocky bed; the hills rising on every side, their slopes covered with forest trees whose foliage had been painted a varied hue by that prince of painters, Jack Frost; the autumn sunshine flooding all with glory, combined to make a picture most entrancing to at least one beholder's eye.

On my way I met an old man and boy, each of whom had been to the well for a jug of water. The former said that he was 76 years of age, and for 25 years he had gone three times a week for the water, and that he had to take no medicine as long as he drank it. It is said that, from April to November, 50 or more people a day visit the well with jugs. A rude sanitarium and natatorium was at one time connected with the well, but it was before the railway entered Corydon, and the facilities for reaching the place were too poor to make it a permanent paying venture. The water had then a high reputation for cures of dyspepsia, rheumatism, chronic neuralgia, scrofula, sore eyes and skin diseases.

At present two old frame buildings, in a bad state of decay, are on the grounds, one of which shelters the well. The water has a distinct, though not strong, odor of hydrogen sulphide. The taste is a combination of bitter, saline and sulphur; the temperature, 63° F. The well is two feet eight inches in diameter, and when cleaned out, a short time before my visit, filled at the rate of four feet in twenty minutes. The grounds and well are owned by three citizens of Corydon, who purchased them a few years ago for $1,600. As noted on page 40, this well is so situated that it could be readily connected with Wyandotte Cave and the White Sulphur Well of Crawford County by electric railway, and a combination of health and pleasure resorts thus effected, which would be unexcelled by any in America.

HENDRICKS COUNTY.

CARTERSBURG MINERAL SPRINGS.

WATER = Neutral.

LOCATION.—One mile north of Cartersburg, a town in the southeastern part of Hendricks County, situated on the Terre Haute and Indianapolis (Vandalia) Railway, 17 miles west of Indianapolis.

ORIGIN AND CHARACTER OF THE WATER.—These springs, which in recent years have gained quite a renown for the purity of their waters and the attractiveness of their surroundings, are six in number. They issue within a few yards of each other, from the base of a gentle slope, facing southward, and lying along the north bank of the West Fork of White Lick Creek. The grounds surrounding the springs are prettily wooded with native sycamore, elm, willow and maple trees, besides a number of cedars and other evergreens. According to tradition, the springs were well known to the Indians, who had one of their villages on the high ground a short distance to the eastward.

A qualitative analysis of the water from the principal spring has been made by Dr. J. N. Hurty, of Indianapolis, who reported on it as follows:

QUALITATIVE ANALYSIS OF MINERAL WATER FROM SPRING NO. 2, CARTERSBURG, INDIANA.

Bases.	Acids.
Magnesium.	Hydrochloric.
Calcium.	Sulphuric.
Iron.	Carbonic.
Sodium.	

Total mineral matter 29.04 grains per U. S. gallon,

VIEWS OF THE CARTERSBURG MINERAL SPRINGS.

PLATE IV.

PORTION OF GROUNDS, CARTERSBURG MINERAL SPRINGS.

LOOKING UP WHITE LICK CREEK FROM CARTERSBURG MINERAL SPRINGS.

"The above bases and acids are combined as chlorides, sulphates and carbonates. The iron exists as carbonate, being rendered soluble by virtue of the presence of a large amount of carbonic acid gas. This gives life and piquancy to the water, and is a valuable medicinal agent, as it makes it grateful to the stomach, relieving nausea and all tenderness. The iron is in very small quantity, which is a matter of unusual moment, because it is found that iron, when taken very dilute, is absorbed and appropriated by the economy, most effectually."—*Hurty*.

In November, 1901, the flow from the three leading springs was about one gallon each per minute. The water was very clear, odorless and tasteless, with a temperature of $53\frac{1}{2}°$ F. In and about one of the springs was a thin deposit of the reddish-brown precipitate of oxide of iron. The water from this spring is probably more truly a chalybeate water than any of the others. The water of a second spring is said to possess magnetic properties. The circular issued by the proprietors claims that the water is a specific for dyspepsia, rheumatism, nervous prostration, general debility, etc.

IMPROVEMENTS.—A company, composed of four prominent citizens of the county, has recently secured control of the springs and 50 acres of surrounding ground. The president of the company, W. R. McClelland, of Danville, is in charge during the season, which is from May 1st to October 1st. About $10,000 have been invested in improvements. These consist of a hotel, comprising three separate buildings, and containing in all 53 well-furnished rooms and a bath house with ten tubs, steam heat, etc. A bowling alley and billiard room furnish facilities for indoor exercise and recreation, while the spacious grounds and the fine roads of the surrounding country afford special advantages for walking and driving.

MARTHA HADLEY MINERAL WELL.

WATER = *Alkaline-saline.*

LOCATION.—On the Martha Hadley farm, northwest quarter Section 25 (15 N., 2 W.), three miles northeast of Amo, a station on the Vandalia Railway, 25 miles west of Indianapolis.

ORIGIN AND CHARACTER OF THE WATER.—A well drilled in the fall of 1902, in search of water for domestic use, was sunk to a depth of 705 feet. In a bluish shale at this depth a strong vein of mineral water was developed, which is said to quickly rust everything made of iron with which it comes in contact. An analysis of the water made by Dr. W. A. Noyes, of Terre Haute, showed its mineral constituents to be as follows:

ANALYSIS OF WATER FROM THE MARTHA HADLEY WELL, NEAR AMO, INDIANA.

Elements and Acid Radicals.	*Grains per U. S. Gallon.*
Silica (SiO₂)................................	0.525
Calcium (Ca)................................	3.442
Magnesium (Mg).............................	1.283
Sodium (Na)................................	151.788
Potassium (K)..............................	1.808
Chlorine (Cl)..............................	230.481
Sulphate (SO₄).............................	0.525
Carbonate (CO₂) (combined).................	9.042
Carbonic acid (H₂CO₃) (free)...............	1.108
Carbonic acid (semi-combined)..............	9.334
Total	409.336

These substances in the water may be considered as being combined as follows:

	Grains per U. S. Gallon.
Silica (SiO₂).................................	0.525
Calcium bi-carbonate (CaH₂(CO₃)₂).............	13.942
Magnesium bi-carbonate (MgH₂(CO₃)₂)..........	7.817
Sodium chloride (NaCl)........................	381.744
Potassium chloride (KCl)......................	0.992
Potassium sulphate (K₂SO₄)....................	0.933
Potassium bi-carbonate (KHCO₃)................	2.275
Carbonic acid (H₂CO₃) (free)..................	1.108
Total	409.336

Besides the above, there were present traces of iron bi-carbonate, barium and strontium sulphates, calcium phosphate, borax, and lithium chloride.

The water is seen to contain quite a large amount of common salt (sodium chloride) and smaller amounts of carbonates of magnesium and lime. It has a salty and somewhat bitter taste, but contains nothing harmful and not much that is very beneficial as a medicinal agent. It is on one of the farms donated by Addison and Martha Hadley to the Women's Christian Temperance Union.

HENRY COUNTY.

SPICELAND MINERAL SPRINGS.

WATER = *Chalybeate.*

LOCATION.—Near the west environs of Spiceland, a town of 600 population, located in the south part of Henry County, on the Ft. Wayne, Cincinnati and Louisville Railway, 29 miles south of Muncie, and two and one-half miles north of Dunreith, a station on the

PLATE V.

SPICELAND SANITARIUM.

AT THE SANITARIUM, WHERE BROOK BEZOR FLOWS.

Pennsylvania Railway, 40 miles east of Indianapolis and 30 miles west of Richmond.

ORIGIN AND CHARACTER OF THE WATER.—Three springs issue a few yards apart from the base of a gentle slope on the eastern side of the three-acre tract owned by the Spiceland Sanitarium Company. A partial analysis of the water has been made by Dr. J. N. Hurty, of Indianapolis, who reported on it as follows: "A qualitative analysis of water from the Mineral Springs at Spiceland, Indiana, shows the presence of the following bases and acids:

Bases.	*Acids.*
Calcium.	Carbonic.
Iron.	Hydrochloric.
Magnesium.	Sulphuric.
Sodium.	

"These bases and acids are combined as carbonates, sulphates and chlorides. This is a chalybeate water, and is very pure, being absolutely free from organic matter.

"The great virtue of the Waukesha water lies in its purity, and not in any mineral matter it contains.

"The Spiceland water has the purity, and also contains iron as a ferrous carbonate, which is considered the most desirable form. This water will be found valuable for all sanitarium purposes."

In September, 1901, the springs had an average flow of three gallons per minute each. The temperature was 54° F. and is said to be the same the year round. The water possesses the characteristic taste of iron carbonate water. No odor of hydrogen sulphide is present. The water is used principally in the sanitarium, both internally and externally. It is claimed to be excellent for rheumatism, stomach, bowel and kidney diseases, and may be used freely.

IMPROVEMENTS.—A sanitarium was erected on the grounds connected with the springs in 1893, and has been open since. Until 1899 the patients were obliged to secure board in private residences of the town, but in that year a hotel, accommodating 30 or more guests, was built, which is open the year round. Facilities for giving mineral water and mud baths are excellent, there being 10 neatly equipped bath rooms. The mud used is a mixture of muck and marl secured from a low spot a short distance south of the sanitarium. The grounds are spacious and well shaded, while pleasant walks and beautiful drives abound in the vicinity.

HOWARD COUNTY.

KOKOMO ARTESIAN WELLS.

WATERS = *Saline-sulphuretted,*
and
Chalybeate.

LOCATION.—In the city park, one mile south of Kokomo, the county seat, a city of 11,000 population, 54 miles north of Indianapolis, on the L. E. & W. Railway. The T., St. L. & W. and the Richmond Division of the Pennsylvania Railway also pass through Kokomo, so that the city is easy of access from all directions. Electric cars run direct to the park.

ORIGIN AND CHARACTER OF THE WATER.—The city park in which the wells are located comprises 42 acres of woodland lying on both sides of Kokomo Creek. It is one of the prettiest small parks in the State, being handsomely laid out and planted with shrubbery and flowers. A large number of natural forest trees and a plentiful water supply add much to its value and beauty. There are said to be five wells in the park which flow under favorable circumstances. Two of them were dry when I was there in August. One I did not find. The main well is located on the north bank of the creek, near the northern end of the park. A five-inch iron casing rises four feet above the surface, and from near its top a flow of mineral water, estimated at four gallons per minute, was escaping from a small pipe. Only a part of the output of the well is allowed to escape at this vent, a portion being piped across the stream to another drinking place.

The water has an agreeable, sweetish saline-sulphur taste, and a distinct odor of hydrogen sulphide. In the rill bearing the overflow into the nearby stream there is a large quantity of the black flakes of iron sulphide, which denote the presence of hydrogen sulphide and iron.

The well is 108 feet in depth, but the mineral water, according to Dr. J. M. Moulder, was struck at 40 feet in a shale. No analysis was available. The water is said to be mildly laxative and an excellent diuretic. It is much used by the citizens of Kokomo.

A second well, flowing about five gallons per minute, of a very pure chalybeate water, is located in a picturesque spot about 200 yards southeast of the one above described. The water bubbles up through an iron pipe into a basin hollowed out in a large boulder, and then flows out through a notch cut in the rim of the basin. It has coated the stone receptacle with the reddish-yellow hue of ferrous oxide, thus proving its chalybeate properties, which are also denoted by the taste. The flow is said to be the same at all seasons.

A third well, 36 feet in depth, located near the south end of the park, is said to yield a copious supply of "lithia" water, but I was unable to secure an analysis from the park commissioners.

The city of Kokomo is to be highly congratulated on having such an excellent and varied supply of mineral waters in its public park, since they are free, and easy of access to all classes of its citizens.

JACKSON COUNTY.

SEYMOUR ARTESIAN WELL.

WATER = *Saline-sulphuretted*.

.LOCATION.—In the southwestern portion of Seymour, a city of 7,000 population, located on the B. & O. S.-W.; Louisville Division of Pennsylvania, and Southern Indiana railways, 46 miles north of Louisville, 64 miles south of Indianapolis, and 88 miles east of Cincinnati.

ORIGIN AND CHARACTER OF THE WATER.—A well sunk for gas on the property of the Seymour Woolen Mills Company, to a depth of 1,140 feet, developed a vein of mineral water in the Niagara limestone at 395 feet. The flow of gas found in Trenton limestone was very small, and was shut off with a plug. The upper casing was left in the well to keep out the surface water, and the mineral water rose and overflowed the top of the casing in a small stream three feet above the surface. A qualitative analysis of it, made by C. T. Fennel, of Cincinnati, showed the presence of sodium chloride, calcium chloride, potassium chloride and calcium carbonate. Hydrogen sulphide is present, but not in such quantity as to make the odor or taste objectionable. The temperature of the water is 55° F. The supply is plentiful, never having been noticeably reduced by pumping. It is much used by the residents of Seymour, both as a beverage and as a remedy for skin and stomach diseases, etc.

IMPROVEMENTS.—A small bath house, equipped with four tubs and with facilities for giving Turkish, Russian and shampoo baths, has been erected near the well. It is open the entire year and is well patronized.

JASPER COUNTY.*

RENSSELAER MINERAL WELLS.

WATER = *Saline-sulphuretted* (?).

LOCATION.—In or near Rensselaer, the county seat, a city of 2,700 population, situated on the C. I. & L. (Monon) Railway, 73 miles south of Chicago.

ORIGIN AND CHARACTER OF THE WATER.—Three wells sunk respectively to depths of 245, 630 and 1,427 feet, have developed veins of mineral water which rises above the surface.

The S. P. Thompson artesian well was sunk in 1868 to a depth of 630 feet. It is located two blocks southwest of the court house. The output, in December, 1901, was three gallons per minute of a clear water, with a distinct odor of hydrogen sulphide and a temperature of 52° F. A white deposit of free sulphur coats objects near the well.

City Water Works Wells.—Two wells, located four blocks northwest of the court house, produce the same quality of water as does the Thompson well. One of these was sunk in 1886, in search of gas, to a depth of 1,427 feet; the other in 1898, to a depth of 245 feet. The output of the two wells, in December, 1901, was about 20 gallons per minute. When pumped, the supply is as large from one as from the other. It is very probable that the water in all three wells comes from a depth of 180 to 210 feet. No analysis of the water has been made.

Besides the above, several shallow wells have been sunk in or near Rensselaer, which produce flowing water containing more or less hydrogen sulphide. These range in depth from 30 to 45 feet, entering the rock at six to fifteen feet. The water comes from the Lockport limestone which underlies the drift.

The Wm. Washburne well, eight blocks west of the court house, has a depth of 36 feet and flows about 75 gallons an hour. The J. D. Babcock well, one-half mile west of the court house, is 45 feet in depth and flows 25 gallons per hour. Both have sufficient hydrogen sulphide in the water to cause a deposit of free sulphur over surrounding objects.

Several springs in the vicinity of Rensselaer produce a similar water. One on the J. D. Babcock farm, one-half mile west, flows 40 gallons per hour, of a water having a temperature of 43° F. Another on the bank of the Iroquois River, 300 feet distant, wells

---

*For much of the data regarding the mineral waters of this county I am indebted to the kindness of Prof. W. O. Hiatt, of Rensselaer.

up in a larger flow through an old barrel which has been sunk about its orifice. Both yield quite an amount of hydrogen sulphide gas, which is doubtless derived by percolation through the limestone above mentioned.

Other springs whose waters are charged with hydrogen sulphide and possibly metallic salts occur in Jasper County as follows: One at Pleasant Ridge, four miles east of Rensselaer; one near McCoysburg, five miles east of Rensselaer; four or five, six miles south, and one four miles northwest. The water of none of these has been analyzed. All are used more or less locally.

Besides hydrogen sulphide, the waters of the wells and springs near Rensselaer doubtless contain other minerals, which only chemical analyses can determine. Such analyses will probably show them to possess medicinal properties of sufficient importance to justify their use in sanitariums.

JEFFERSON COUNTY.

AUSTIN MINERAL WATER WELL.

WATER = *Saline.*

LOCATION.—On the farm of Dr. F. H. Austin, near North Madison, a station on the Madison Branch of the Pennsylvania Railway, two miles north of Madison, and 84 miles southeast of Indianapolis.

ORIGIN AND CHARACTER OF THE WATER.—The well which yields the water was bored for oil or gas in 1890 to a depth of 1,500 feet. At about 1,450 feet mineral water was struck, which rose to within 200 feet of the surface. A qualitative analysis by Prof. A. H. Young, of Hanover, showed the presence of the following acids and bases:

ANALYSIS OF MINERAL WATER FROM NORTH MADISON GAS WELL.

Bases.	*Acids.*
Calcium (plentiful).	Sulphuric acid (plentiful).
Magnesium (considerable amount).	Carbonic acid (not excessive, but
Iron (small amount).	enough to form bi-carbonates of
Potassium (small amount).	calcium, magnesium and iron).
Sodium (very plentiful).	Hydrochloric acid (plentiful).
Lithium (faint traces).	Phosphoric acid (very small
Magnesium (trace).	amount).
	Silicic acid (small amount).

The water is used locally, but not extensively.

JOHNSON COUNTY.

GREENWOOD MINERAL WELL.

WATER = *Saline-sulphuretted* (?).

LOCATION.—Near the eastern limits of Greenwood, a town of 1,600 population, situated on the Louisville and Indianapolis Division of the Pennsylvania Railway, 11 miles south of Indianapolis. The well is located within one block of the railway station and four blocks east of the line of the Indianapolis, Greenwood and Franklin Electric Railway.

ORIGIN AND CHARACTER OF THE WATER.—The well producing the mineral water was sunk in 1894 to a depth of 1,725 feet. The bore passed entirely through the Trenton limestone and about 25 feet into the St. Peter's sandstone. Here a vein of water was struck which arose to within 325 feet of the surface. This water resembles very closely that found at Shelbyville in the same formation. Only a qualitative analysis, by Dr. J. N. Hurty, of Indianapolis, has been made. He reports the presence of the following elements:

Bases.	*Acid Radicals.*
Sodium.	Hydrochloric.
Magnesium.	Sulphuric.
Calcium.	Carbonic.
Iron.	Silicic.
Aluminum.	Hydro-sulphuric.

The water, as raised by steam pump, is quite black with flakes of iron sulphide. The odor of sulphuretted hydrogen is present, but weak. The taste is quite saline, but not bitter, and when diluted one-half with pure water, is very agreeable. The temperature of the water as pumped is 56° F.

IMPROVEMENTS.—A short time after the well was completed a two-story frame sanitarium and bath house was erected by the Greenwood Sanitarium Company, composed of citizens of the town and vicinity. It is located just northwest of the well, on a tract of six acres, which has been planted to shade trees and shrubbery. The building is steam heated and contains, besides reception rooms and offices, 20 bath rooms equipped with porcelain-lined tubs, and also facilities for giving vapor and shower baths. The well opens into a brick building adjoining, in which are engines and pumps; also tanks, in which the water is held and from which it is piped into the sanitarum. The town of Greenwood is situated in a fine agricultural community, with good roads radiating in all directions.

BRADLEY MINERAL SPRING.

WATER = *Chalybeate.*

LOCATION.—On the Forest Ridge farm, about seven miles south of Franklin, the county seat.

ORIGIN AND CHARACTER OF THE WATER.—A spring emerges from the black Devonian shale on the south side of Sugar Creek, about midway between the State Road and the railway. It flows about 75 gallons an hour, of a clear, cold water, which tastes strongly of iron oxide. The spring has built up a large mound of ferruginous, carbonaceous material below its original outlet, and flows over the top of this mound, the size of which is slowly increasing by deposits from the water. No analysis has been made. The water has quite a large local use.

* * *

In the report of this department for 1883, page 133, Rev. David S. McCaslin makes the following mention of another group of mineral springs which I did not find time to visit:

"The finest and most noted mineral springs (in Johnson County) are found in Section 7, Nineveh Township. They are known as the 'Vickerman Springs,' after the name of the original owner of the land. They are three in number, all close together and issuing from the base of a boldly escarped bluff of bowlder drift. The springs flow out at the top of the sandstone strata at the base of the clay. They are quite similar in character, though the one farthest to the west exhibits the most decided mineral character. Its analysis was not obtained. The water is said to have medicinal properties, and many have testified as to its efficacy in certain disorders. It has a pleasant taste. The rocks over which it flows are colored bluish black, as is the whole bed of the stream into which it flows, for some distance below. Bubbles issuing occasionally, indicate the presence of a free gas."

KOSCIUSKO COUNTY.

WINONA MINERAL SPRINGS.

WATER = *Alkaline.*

LOCATION.—In the west half of Section 15 (32 N., 6 E.), just east of the Winona Assembly grounds, on the eastern shore of Eagle or Winona Lake. Two miles east of Warsaw, the county seat, a city of 4,000 population, situated at the crossing of the Pittsburg, Ft. Wayne and Chicago and the Michigan Division of the Big Four railways, 109 miles east of Chicago, 122 miles north of Indianapolis.

ORIGIN AND CHARACTER OF THE WATER.—A number of springs issue along the base of a low range of wooded hills composed of drift material, which form the eastern rim of the basin in which the waters of Eagle Lake are held. The lake is in part fed by the waters of these springs.

The water as it issues is clear, cold and sparkling; odorless and tasteless. An analysis by Dr. R. E. Lyons, of Bloomington, Indiana, showed the mineral ingredients present to be as follows:

ANALYSIS OF WATER FROM WINONA SPRINGS.

Grains per U. S. Gallon.

Potassium chloride (KCl)	.0495
Sodium chloride (NaCl)	.3411
Sodium nitrate (NaNO$_3$)	.0350
Sodium sulphate (Na$_2$SO$_4$)	.3224
Calcium sulphate (CaSO$_4$)	3.6493
Calcium bi-carbonate (CaH$_2$(CO$_3$)$_2$)	15.5420
Magnesium bi-carbonate (MgH$_2$(CO$_3$)$_2$)	8.4868
Ferrous carbonate (FeCO$_3$)	.1294
Alumina (Al$_2$O$_3$)	.0524
Silica (SiO$_2$)	.7523
Total solids	29.3602

The analysis shows a very pure, slightly alkaline or neutral water. It has been used many years by persons living in the vicinity, and since the Winona Association secured control of the grounds, by thousands of summer visitors. That association has ceded for 20 years the right to bottle and ship this water to a company known as the Winona Springs Company. A bottling works, with a capacity for bottling and charging with carbon-dioxide 26,000 gallons of water daily, was erected in 1901. To a part of the water lithium oxide is also added, and the water is sold under the name of "Winona Lithia Water." The purity and sparkling qualities of the water will recommend it highly for table use.

LAKE COUNTY.

HAMMOND ARTESIAN WELLS.

WATER = *Alkaline-saline.*

LOCATION.—In and near the boundaries of the city of Hammond, located within three miles of the south shore of Lake Michigan, in the northwestern corner of the county, 21 miles southeast of Chicago. Seven railways furnish outlet in all directions. Population in 1900, 12,376.

ORIGIN AND CHARACTER OF THE WATER.—Six wells sunk to depths of 1,840 to 1,875 feet, have in the past furnished an artesian flow of mineral water at Hammond. For a time this water was used for domestic purposes, and at several of the larger factories, but its use has in recent years been displaced by the public water supply from Lake Michigan. In October, 1901, most of the wells had ceased flowing, having been stopped up, it was claimed, by an accumulation of mineral salts; but if necessity required, they could be easily opened, thus renewing the flow. Two of them were located on the grounds of the Western Starch Association. A chemical analysis of the water from one of these, which will probably hold good for that formerly flowing from the other five, showed the presence of the following solids:

ANALYSIS OF ARTESIAN WATER FROM WESTERN STARCH ASSOCIATION WELL, HAMMOND, INDIANA.

	Grains per U. S. Gallon.
Calcium carbonate ($CaCO_3$)	10.003
Magnesium carbonate ($MgCO_3$)	9.283
Sodium sulphate (Na_2SO_4)	29.894
Sodium chloride ($NaCl$)	20.913
Sodium carbonate (Na_2CO_3)	3.260
Calcium sulphate ($CaSO_4$)	38.308
Silica (SiO_2)	1.022
Oxide of iron and alumina ($Fe_2O_3+Al_2O_3$)	.058
Total solids	112.741

WILLOWDALE SPRINGS.

WATER = Alkaline.

LOCATION.—On the Willowdale Stock Farm, owned by W. J. Davis, one-half mile north of Crown Point, the county seat, a town of 2,500 population, situated 36 miles southeast from Chicago on the Chicago and Erie and the P., C., C. & St. L. railways.

ORIGIN AND CHARACTER OF THE WATER.—Two springs issue a few rods apart from the base of a knoll, the surface of which is eight or ten feet higher than the surrounding land.

An analysis made for the owner by Dr. T. C. Van Nuys, formerly chemist at the State University, showed the mineral constituents to be as follows:

ANALYSIS OF WATER FROM WILLOWDALE SPRINGS, NEAR CROWN POINT, INDIANA.

Grains per U. S. Gallon.

Potassium sulphate (K_2SO_4)............................ .799
Sodium sulphate (Na_2SO_4)............................. .113
Sodium carbonate (Na_2CO_3)........................... 1.398
Sodium chloride (NaCl)................................ .183
Aluminum sulphate ($Al_2(SO_4)_3$)...................... .652
Calcium bi-carbonate ($CaH_2(CO_3)_2$)................19.290
Magnesium bi-carbonate ($MgH_2(CO_3)_2$)...............11.650
Silicic acid ($Si(OH)_4$).................................. 1.664

Total solids 35.749

The analysis shows this to be an alkaline water of excellent quality. It is clear and sparkling. The flow at the two springs combined is about 12 gallons per minute. It has not, as yet, been used to any extent for medicinal purposes.

* * *

At East Chicago, a city of 3,500 inhabitants, in the northern part of Lake County, there is an artesian well 1,830 feet in depth, which yields a copious supply of an excellent chalybeate water. The natural pressure is sufficient to raise the water 40 feet above the surface.

LAPORTE COUNTY.

MICHIGAN CITY ARTESIAN WELLS.

LOCATION.—Three wells yielding an artesian flow of mineral water are found in the immediate vicinity of Michigan City. One is located on the grounds of the Northern Penitentiary, one mile southwest of the city; a second well is on the lake front, between the penitentiary and Lake Michigan, while the third is two miles southwest of the city, in the edge of Porter County.

Michigan City has a population of 15,000. It is located on a good harbor on the southeastern border of Lake Michigan, 56 miles east of Chicago and 161 miles northwest of Indianapolis. The Michigan Central, Monon and L. E. & W. railways furnish easy access from all directions.

(a) NORTHERN PENITENTIARY WELL.

WATER = *Alkaline-saline-sulphuretted* (?).

ORIGIN AND CHARACTER OF THE WATER.—The first of these flowing wells was put down to a depth of $541\frac{1}{2}$ feet within the walls of the penitentiary 30 years or more ago. Dr. G. M. Levette, in the report of this department for 1873, p. 470, gives the following account of this well, which I quote verbatim, as no later information is available. "The bore terminates in a porous (Niagara) limestone rock, from which flows a stream of mineral water, strongly impregnated with sulphuretted hydrogen. The water rises twenty-two feet above the surface of the ground, discharges at the rate of about 300 gallons per minute and has a temperature of 57° F.

"A qualitative analysis of the water was made, by a chemist in Chicago, at the request of the prison authorities, which indicated the presence of the following constituents:

> Carbonate of lime.
> Bi-carbonate of magnesia.
> Bi-carbonate of soda.
> Bi-carbonate of potash.
> Sulphate of soda.
> Chloride of sodium.
> Chloride of potassium.

"The water gives an alkaline reaction and is strongly charged with sulphuretted hydrogen and carbonic acid gas. It is a decided alterative and may prove remedial in diseases of the liver, kidneys and skin."

Since the above was in press, I have learned from Warden Reid that the well is now plugged, but the plug can be easily removed and the flow renewed at any time.

(b) ZORN ARTESIAN WELL.

WATERS = *Alkaline-saline,*
and
Saline-sulphuretted.

ORIGIN AND CHARACTER OF THE WATER.—This well, located on the lake front, southwest of the city, and owned by Mr. Philip Zorn, was sunk in 1899 to a depth of 950 feet. At 292 feet, in a Devonian shale, a flow of strong "blue lick" sulphur water was encountered. At 387 feet, in the Niagara limestone, a second vein of so-called "white sulphur" water was developed, while at a depth of 630 feet a third vein of more strongly saline water was found. The three veins of water flow through separate pipes from the surface, the total output approximating 70 gallons per minute.

An analysis of the water from the lower vein, made for the owner by Frank Gazzolo, a Chicago chemist, resulted as follows:

ANALYSIS OF WATER FROM ZORN ARTESIAN WELL, MICHIGAN CITY, INDIANA.

Grains per U. S. Gallon.

Potassium nitrate (KNO_3)	.16
Potassium chloride (KCl)	12.31
Sodium chloride (NaCl)	356.68
Ammonium chloride (NH_4Cl)	1.41
Magnesium chloride ($MgCl_2$)	87.28
Calcium chloride ($CaCl_2$)	82.50
Calcium sulphate ($CaSO_4$)	134.71
Calcium carbonate ($CaCO_3$)	1.98
Oxide of iron and alumina (Fe_2O_3&Al_2O_3)	.20
Silica (SiO_2)	.17
Total solids	677.40

This is a true saline water, free from the odor and taste of hydrogen sulphide. The upper two veins, of which no analyses have been made, both contain gaseous hydrogen sulphide in sufficient quantity to emit a strong odor. The flow from the uppermost (292 feet) is much the stronger and has a temperature of 56° F. The well is located in a beautiful natural park, one and a half miles from the center of the city. Pine and oak trees cover the high sand dunes, which in themselves are objects of interest to many persons from a distance. The site is an ideal one for a great sanitarium, the proximity of the lake furnishing bathing and fishing facilities not often present in connection with good mineral waters.

The water from the well is free to all who apply, and is used extensively by the residents of Michigan City, with beneficial results for kidney and liver complaints and for skin diseases.

(c) BLAIR ARTESIAN WELL.

WATER = *Alkaline-saline-sulphuretted.*

ORIGIN AND CHARACTER OF THE WATER.—This well was sunk about 1875 to a depth of 858 feet. It is located in the extreme northeastern corner of Porter County, north half of Section 1 (37 N., 5 W.), two miles southwest of Michigan City. A strong vein of mineral water was developed in the Niagara limestone, which has continued to flow with unabated force. An analysis, made by Dr. P. S. Hays, of the Chicago College of Pharmacy, showed the presence of the following mineral salts:

ANALYSIS OF ARTESIAN WATER FROM BLAIR WELL, NEAR MICHIGAN CITY, INDIANA.

Grains per U. S. Gallon.

Sodium chloride (NaCl)	360.4794
Magnesium chloride (MgCl₂)	45.6550
Potassium sulphate (K₂SO₄)	17.9968
Magnesium sulphate (MgSO₄)	31.9730
Calcium sulphate (CaSO₄)	84.4024
Calcium bi-carbonate (CaH₂(CO₃)₂)	147.8503
Silica (SiO₂)	1.7523
Total solids	690.1092

A bath house and sanitarium were erected soon after the well was' finished. For a number of years the place was well patronized, and the majority of the guests were highly benefited by the use of the water. Since the death of the owner, the use of the water has been practically abandoned and the improvements have fallen into decay.

The water rushes forth at the rate of 180 gallons per minute. It has a strong odor of hydrogen sulphide and the characteristic white deposit of sulphur from this gas coats many objects near the orifice of the well. Taking into consideration the excellent qualities of the water and its location so near the shores of Lake Michigan, it would seem that under the proper management a summer resort and sanitarium could be so combined as to make a valuable and paying property of this well.

LAWRENCE COUNTY.

AVOCA MINERAL SPRING.

WATER = *Saline-sulphuretted.*

LOCATION.—In the town of Avoca, five miles northwest of Bedford, on the Switz City Branch of the Monon Railway. Bedford, the county seat, from which the spring can be easily reached by hack or private carriage, is a city of 6,500 inhabitants, on the Monon, Southern Indiana and branch of the B. & O. S.-W. railways, 134 miles east of Cincinnati and 77 miles north of Louisville.

ORIGIN AND CHARACTER OF THE WATER.—The spring which yields the mineral water at Avoca emerges from the base of a stratum of Harrodsburg limestone on the east branch of Goose Creek, Section 31 (6 N., 1 W.). It is located at the rear of the general merchandise store of D. E. Bennett, to whom it belongs. A basin 24x18 inches in size and 18 inches deep has been excavated in the stone, and then cemented. When emptied, this is said to fill in 30 minutes, making the flow about 70 gallons per hour. The water is clear and sparkling, and has a temperature of 62° F. The flow and temperature are said to be the same at all seasons. The water emits a strong odor of hydrogen sulphide and has a slightly bitter taste. A white precipitate of sulphur occurs in the rill bearing away the overflow, and the spring is, for that reason, known locally as the "White Sulphur" Spring. No analysis of its waters has been made. It has quite a local reputation for diseases of the skin, sore eyes, and for kidney and bladder diseases. At the time of my visit the surroundings were in bad condition.

According to Hayden Bridwell, a prominent and intelligent citizen of Avoca, a number of similar springs, though with a smaller flow, emerge along Goose Creek both above and below the town.

FELDUN FIELDS MINERAL WELLS.

WATER = *Alkaline-saline-sulphuretted.*

LOCATION.—About four miles northwest of Bedford and three-quarters of a mile west of Avoca, on the land of the Misses Fell, of Bedford.

ORIGIN AND CHARACTER OF THE WATER.—A few years ago, while core drilling for oolitic stone, Hon. Moses Dunn, of Bedford, developed flowing mineral water in three wells on the land mentioned. One of the wells is 45 feet deep and the water rises about six feet above the surface. The other two are respectively 75 feet and 100 feet in depth. They are located about 1,000 feet apart. The water. was found at the base of the blue oolitic limestone, probably in the Harrodsburg limestone, which is the source of a similar water at the Avoca "White Sulphur" Spring.

An analysis of the water from one of the Feldun Field wells was made by Dr. Robert E. Lyons, Professor of Chemistry at Indiana University, who reported on it as follows:

ANALYSIS OF MINERAL WATER FROM WELL NO. 5, FELDUN FIELDS, LAWRENCE COUNTY, INDIANA.

The following is the number of parts of each constituent in 10,000 parts of water:

Sulphur as free sulphuretted hydrogen................ 0.0846
Sulphur as hyposulphites............................. 0.0150
Sulphur as sulphates................................. 0.6361

Sulphur as sulphides................................... 0.1665
Silica (SiO_2)... 0.1230
Chlorine (Cl)... 1.3647
Potassium oxide (K_2O).............................. 0.0483
Sodium oxide (Na_2O)................................ 1.5462
Ferric oxide (Fe_2O_3).............................. 0.0471
Aluminum oxide (Al_2O_3)........................... 0.0222
Calcium oxide (CaO)................................... 0.9584
Magnesium oxide (MgO)................................ 0.8390
Carbon dioxide (CO_2).............................. 3.9685
Lithium oxide (Li_2O).............................. trace

The constituents are probably in the following combinations:

	Grains per U. S. Gallon.
Potassium hyposulphite ($K_2S_2O_3$)........................	.266
Potassium sulphide (K_2S)............................	.170
Sodium sulphide (Na_2S)............................	2.247
Sodium chloride (NaCl)................................	12.387
Magnesium sulphate ($MgSO_4$)........................	13.910
Magnesium chloride ($MgCl_2$)........................	.640
Calcium bi-carbonate ($Ca(HCO_3)_2$).................	16.160
Ferrous bi-carbonate ($Fe(HCO_3)_2$).................	7.048
Aluminum silicate ($Al_2(SIO_3)_3$)..................	.353
Silica (SiO_2)......................................	.567
Lithium carbonate (Li_2CO_3).......................	trace
Total solids	53.748

Gases.	Cu. In.
Carbon di-oxide (free) (CO_2)........................	21.43
Sulphuretted hydrogen (free) (H_2S)................	1.56

"The water is clear, colorless, and has a strong odor and taste of sulphuretted hydrogen gas. Its temperature is 52.1° F.

"By standing in contact with the air the water becomes cloudy and finally slightly yellow in color, owing to the separation of sulphur and the formation of higher sulphides of the alkali metals.

"By boiling, the water becomes turbid from the decomposition of the bi-carbonates of calcium and magnesium. The water after boiling has a bitter saline taste. This is to be explained by the fact that the sulphuretted hydrogen and the free and loosely combined carbon dioxide are separated and expelled during the process of boiling. This saline water will prove diuretic, laxative, alterative and resolvent."—*Lyons.*

* * *

Several other springs occur in Lawrence County whose waters are quite similar to those above mentioned. One on the estate of Dr.

Denson, one mile southwest of Bedford, is strongly charged with hydrogen sulphide, and is used extensively by the citizens of Bedford. The flow, however, is weak, probably 10 gallons an hour.

A number of others bubble up in the bed of Indian Creek in the southeast quarter Section 17 (5 N., 2 W.), near the old Gray's mill.

MARION COUNTY.

MT. JACKSON SANITARIUM.

WATER = *Saline-sulphuretted.*

LOCATION.—At Nos. 3127-3129 West Washington Street, Indianapolis, Indiana, three miles west of the center of the city. The West Washington Street electric cars pass the door every ten minutes, and connect at the Indianapolis Union Station with trains in all directions.

ORIGIN AND CHARACTER OF THE WATER.—A six-inch bore sunk in 1899 to a depth of 1,541 feet, developed, in the St. Peter's sandstone, a strong vein of mineral water, which filled the bore to within 150 feet of the top. The supply is inexhaustible, and is raised by a steam pump and piped through the adjacent sanitarium. An analysis of the water by T. W. Smith, of Indianapolis, shows its mineral constituents to be as follows:

ANALYSIS OF WATER FROM THE MT. JACKSON MINERAL WELL.

	Grains per U. S. Gallon.
Silica (SiO_2)	0.980
Sodium chloride (NaCl) } Potassium chloride (KCl) }	646.800
Calcium sulphate ($CaSO_4$)	1.300
Calcium carbonate ($CaCO_3$)	20.000
Calcium chloride ($CaCl_2$)	102.600
Magnesium carbonate ($MgCO_3$)	24.200
Magnesium chloride ($MgCl_2$)	140.000
Total	935.880
	Cu. In.
Hydrogen sulphide gas (H_2S)	4.270

The water has a very pleasant, sweetish-saline taste. When first pumped it is often dark-colored or milky, owing to the compounds of sulphur present, but after standing a short time becomes clear and limpid. The hydrogen sulphide gas is not present in sufficient quantity to render either the odor or the taste disagreeable. The specific gravity is, according to Smith, 1.011, and the temperature 60° F. In the sanitarium it is used extensively for bathing purposes and also internally for stomach troubles. It is claimed to be a sovereign remedy for rheumatism and skin diseases, and an excellent blood purifier. Many of the leading physicians of Indianapolis send patients to the sanitarium for the baths and hundreds of citizens are regular patrons at all seasons.

The water is bottled and shipped in small quantities, being sold at $1.80 per dozen quarts, or 25 cents per gallon in jugs.

IMPROVEMENTS.—A two-story brick and stone building is used as a sanitarium and bath house. It is steam-heated and contains 20 neatly furnished rooms for guests and 17 well-equipped bath rooms. The location, within ten minutes' ride of the theaters and other amusement centers of the city, will allow the necessary recreation for guests from a distance.

NEWHAVEN WELL.

WATER = *Neutral.*

LOCATION.—One and a quarter miles northeast of Lawrence, a station on the lines of the Cleveland Division of the Big Four Railway and the Union Traction Company of Indiana, eight miles northeast of Indianapolis. Both lines of railway run alongside the grove in which the well is located.

ORIGIN AND CHARACTER OF THE WATER.—A well dug, in 1898, to a depth of 29 feet in the drift, yields a plentiful supply of clear, odorless water, which has a slightly bitter taste and a temperature of 50° F. A partial analysis of the water, made by T. W. Smith, of Indianapolis, developed the presence of very small amounts of calcium and magnesium sulphates, and traces only of potassium, iron and chlorine. The water is, therefore, to be classed as neutral and pure. The well is located on the east side of a very pretty walnut and hickory grove and the water is raised to the surface by a wooden pump.

MARTIN COUNTY.

TRINITY SPRINGS.

WATER = *Saline-sulphuretted.*

LOCATION.—On the northwest quarter Section 28 (4 N., 3 W.), seven miles northeast of Shoals, the county seat, and three miles southeast of Indian Springs, a station on the Southern Indiana Railway. The property on which the springs are located, consisting of 280 acres, has recently been acquired by John R. Walsh, of Chicago, the owner of the Southern Indiana, who proposes building a branch to within a short distance of the springs. Postoffice, Trinity Springs.

ORIGIN AND CHARACTER OF THE WATER.—"Trinity Springs," so called from their number, are among the oldest and best known "sulphur springs" of the State. Three springs well up from rifts or crevices in the Mansfield sandstone rock. A ridge, finely wooded with native forest trees, rises 30 or more feet above the springs to the east. Two of these springs are but eight feet apart; the other about 20 feet south. The middle spring produces about 50 gallons of water per minute; the one to the north about 10 gallons, while the output of the southern one approximates 30 gallons per minute. The water is clear; the odor of hydrogen sulphide strong; the taste not disagreeable, being but slightly bitter and sulphuretted. In the rivulets bearing away the overflow there are heavy precipitates of black sulphide of iron and whitish free sulphur. The temperature of the water is $56\frac{1}{2}°$ F. at all seasons.

Three analyses have been made of the waters of these springs. One, by Mr. John F. Elsom, in 1883, was published in Dr. Peale's paper.[*] A second, made by Dr. T. C. Van Nuys, of Bloomington, in 1890, has since been incorporated in circulars sent out by the proprietors. A third was made in 1899 by Mariner & Hoskins, analytical chemists, at 81 South Clark Street, Chicago. Of these analyses, that of Dr. Van Nuys is the only one which shows the percentage of the bases and acid radicals present. These, as given by him, were expressed in "parts of mineral matter per 1,000 parts of water," as follows:

ANALYSIS OF WATER FROM TRINITY SPRINGS, BY DR. T. C. VAN NUYS.

Sulphur combined as sulphuretted hydrogen	0.0103840
Sulphur combined as hyposulphites	0.0060864
Sulphur combined as metallic sulphides	0.0003344
Sulphur combined as sulphates of metals	0.5103608
Carbon dioxide	0.1635000
Chlorine	0.1575600
Silica	0.0114000
Calcium oxide	0.7057000
Magnesium oxide	0.2028828
Potassium oxide	0.0443617
Sodium oxide	0.1535128

The compounds of mineral salts present, according to the views of each of the three chemists, are shown in the following table:

---

[*] Bulletin 32, U. S. Geological Survey, 1886, p. 139.

PLATE VI.

TRINITY SPRINGS, MARTIN COUNTY, INDIANA.

ANALYSES OF WATERS FROM TRINITY SPRINGS, INDIANA.

	ELSOM.	VAN NUYS.	MARINER & HOSKINS.
		Grains per U. S. Gallon.	
Potassium hyposulphite...........	.....	1.054	.....
Potassium sulphide...............	.....	.067	.....
Sodium chloride..................	8.338	15.140	.....
Sodium silicate..................	.....	1.352	.....
Calcium sulphate................	1.26	99.934	71.07
Magnesium sulphate.............	4.165	23.430	14.71
Sodium bi-carbonate.............	.116	.655	.....
Potassium bi-carbonate...........	.067	4.273	.....
Magnesium carbonate............	4.107	8.450	.....
Calcium carbonate...............	5.589	.....	5.84
Magnesium chloride.............	1.099	.....	14.83
Sodium sulphate.................	.350	.....	32.82
Potassium sulphate...............	.097	.....	.....
Calcium chloride.................	.708	.....	.....
Silica	.825	.....	.....
Totals	26.721	154.355	139.27

Gases.		Cu. In.	Cu. In.
Hydrogen sulphide...............	.....	1.721	1.09
Carbon dioxide..................	.....	5.78	.....

The analysis of Mr. Elsom differs so widely from the other two that it is manifestly wrong.

The percentages of bases and acid radicals as found by Messrs. Mariner & Hoskins probably differed but little from those found by Dr. Van Nuys. A difference of opinion as to the character of the resulting compounds accounts for the difference in analyses as shown in the table. Dr. Van Nuys added the following remarks to his analysis as given: "This is a saline sulphuretted water and in the amount of sulphur contained in it compares favorably with many of the noted sulphur springs of Germany, the amount of sulphuretted hydrogen contained being above the average. The absence of aluminum, iron and the nitrates is to be noted. The specific gravity of the water is 1.0019."

IMPROVEMENTS.—Trinity Springs were first opened to the public about 60 years ago. A large hotel, which was built for the accommodation of the visitors, was burned in 1863. Since then the patrons have found accommodations in the hotels and private houses of Harrisonville, a small town a third of a mile west. A fine grove occupies a portion of the terrace or second bottom of Indian Creek, which lies between the springs and that stream. This grove is used as a park and as a place for tennis courts, croquet grounds, etc. A portion of it is also utilized by campers, many of whom visit the springs each year. A small bath house is located at the eastern edge of the grove, where private baths can be taken in water piped from the spring. It is understood that Mr. Walsh, the new owner, will spend a large sum in improvements. The quantity and quality of the water; the picturesqueness and quiet of the surroundings, will, without doubt, bring to these springs a host of visitors as soon as the long needed accommodations and means of access have been provided.

INDIAN SPRINGS.

WATER = *Alkaline-saline-sulphuretted.*

LOCATION.—Eight miles north of Shoals, the county seat, and one mile southeast of Indian Springs, a station on the Southern Indiana Railway, 66 miles southeast of Terre Haute.

ORIGIN AND CHARACTER OF THE WATER.—Mineral water from a vein a few feet below the surface, wells up at four different places within a few yards of one another on the west bank of Sulphur Creek, west half of Section 17 (4 N., 3 W.). In October, 1901, these springs were being improved by sinking sections of sewer pipe about their orifices. One iron pipe, 12 feet in length and four feet in diameter, had been sunk about the main spring and in this pipe the water was standing within a few inches of the surface. In the others the old sycamore gums, sunk 30 years ago, were still present. There was no perceptible flow from any of the springs, the water standing at a certain height in the pipe or gums. When dipped out, however, it is said to be renewed from below at the rate of about eight gallons per minute in the main spring, down to two gallons in the smaller ones. The water in each comes from the same source or vein, and there is no difference in its appearance or component mineral parts. The temperature of each spring was 57° F. The odor of hydrogen sulphide was perceptible but not strong. The taste is slightly bitter and plainly sulphuretted.

Three analyses of the water from these springs have been made in the past; one by E. T. Cox in 1870*; a second by T. C. Van Nuys in 1892, and a third by Mariner & Hoskins, of Chicago, in 1899. Professor Cox gave the percentage composition of the bases and acid radicals present as follows:

*Geological Survey of Indiana, 1870, p. 108.

PLATE VII.

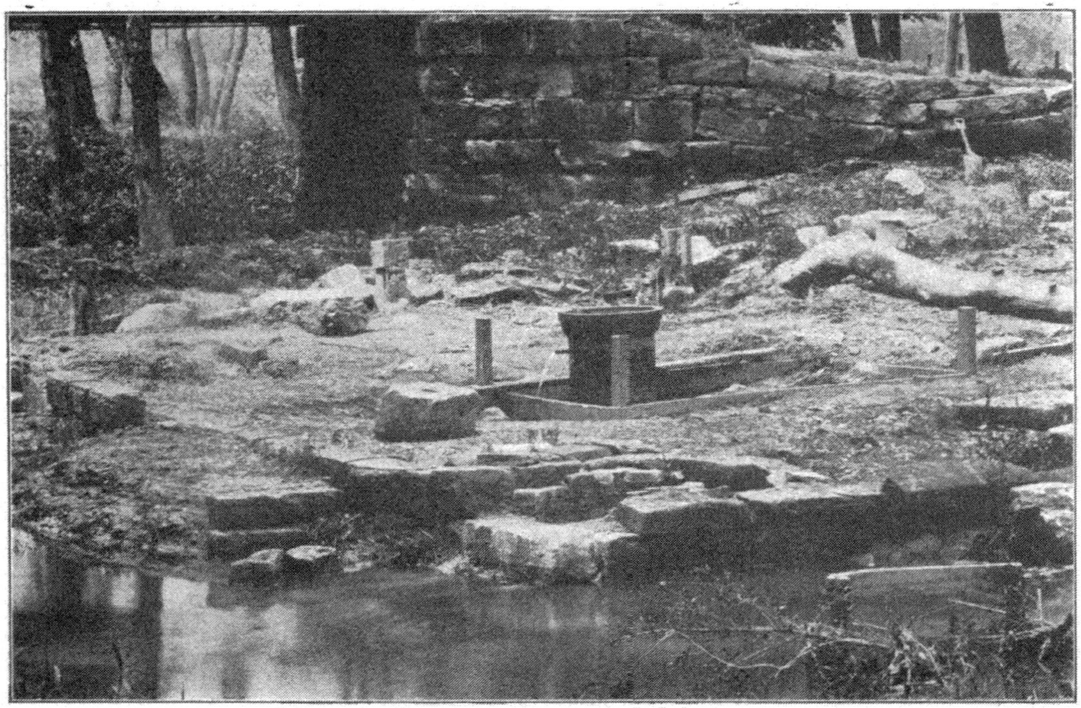

INDIAN SPRINGS, MARTIN COUNTY, INDIANA.

ANALYSIS OF WATER FROM INDIAN SPRINGS, BY E. T. COX.

	Grains per U. S. Gallon.
Silicic acid	.4399
Ferrous oxide	.0065
Lime	22.9279
Soda	27.5356
Potash	2.0658
Magnesia	20.0663
Alumina	.1763
Chlorine	18.5360
Carbonic acid	31.2783
Sulphuric acid	40.5842
Total	163.6138

The probable compounds present, according to the views of each chemist, are as follows:

	COX.	MARINER & HOSKINS.	VAN NUYS.
	Grains per U. S. Gallon.		
Sodium sulphate (Na_2SO_4)	11.828	18.65	.....
Potassium sulphate (K_2SO_4)	2.402	.....	.212
Magnesium sulphate ($MgSO_4$)	30.385	25.46	23.808
Aluminum sulphate ($Al_2(SO_4)_3$)	.829	.....	1.195
Ferrous sulphate ($FeSO_4$)	20.230	.....	.....
Calcium sulphate ($CaSO_4$)	.....	24.82	35.085
Calcium carbonate ($CaCO_3$)	33.102	8.76	12.435
Sodium carbonate (Na_2CO_3)	3.612	.....	.....
Potassium carbonate (K_2CO_3)	2.407	.....	.....
Magnesium carbonate ($MgCO_3$)	18.944	trace	3.218
Manganese carbonate ($MnCO_3$)	.....	.....	.233
Sodium chloride (NaCl)	39.366	.....	1.364
Magnesium chloride ($MgCl_2$)	.056	1.40	1.074
Potassium chloride (KCl)	.....	.....	1.737
Lithium chloride (LiCl)	.....	.....	.020
Calcium chloride ($CaCl_2$)	.....	.....	1.294
Sodium sulphide (Na_2S)	.....	.....	2.555
Sodium silicate (Na_2SiO_3)	.....	.....	1.078
Sodium phosphate (Na_3PO_4)	.....	.....	.127
Silica (SiO_2)	.4399	.....	.....
Ferrous oxide (FeO)	.0035	.....	.003
Total solids	163.6044	79.09	85.438
Gases.	Cu. In.	Cu. In.	Cu. In.
Carbonic acid	9.58	.....	.....
Hydrogen sulphide	3.33	1.66	2.03

How Professor Cox could have only .0035 grains of ferrous oxide in his table of elementary substances, the same amount in his table of compounds and yet have, in addition, in the latter, 20.230 grains of ferrous sulphate, passeth understanding.

HISTORY AND IMPROVEMENTS.—The water of Indian Springs has, in the past, gained a high reputation for its medicinal virtues. These springs are said to have been in high repute among the Indians, and to have been opened to the public as a health resort in 1814. For a long time a large two-story frame hotel stood on the crest of the hill which rises 86 feet above the springs on the east. This was torn down in 1900 to make room for a more pretentious structure which Mr. Walsh, the new owner, proposes building. The site is a fine one, overlooking a wide and picturesque valley to the east and south. The slope which leads gradually from the hotel site down to the springs, is finely wooded with beech, oak, maple, locust, cedar and other trees. A railway switch in course of construction from the Southern Indiana, will bring passengers right to the springs. Since Mr. Walsh has gained control of Trinity Springs to the southeast and the intervening wooded territory, a combined resort, unexcelled in the State, will probably be established.

LA SALLE SPRING.

WATER = *Alkaline-saline-sulphuretted.* ·

LOCATION.—On the north bank of the east fork of White River, northeast quarter Section 22 (4 N., 3 W.), two miles northeast of Trinity Springs. Five miles from Indian Springs and three miles from Mt. Olive, stations on the Southern Indiana Railway; four miles from Huron and 10 miles from Shoals on the B. & O. S.-W. Railway. Telephonic connection with Shoals and Bedford. Postoffice, Mt. Olive.

ORIGIN AND CHARACTER OF THE WATER.—A strong flowing spring of "white sulphur" water issues from the foot of the river bluff, about 15 feet above low water mark, and flows over limestone rocks about 30 feet into the river. At high water the river covers these rocks and reaches the mouth of the spring. An analysis of the water by Dr. Louis Schmidt, of the Cincinnati Department of Health, shows its composition to be as follows:

ANALYSIS OF WATER FROM LASALLE SPRING, MARTIN COUNTY, INDIANA.

	Grains per U. S. Gallon.
Calcium carbonate ($CaCO_3$)	36.680
Ferrous carbonate ($FeCO_3$)	.232
Calcium sulphate ($CaSO_4$)	46.408
Magnesium sulphate ($MgSO_4$)	81.472

PLATE VIII.

TRINITY SPRINGS, MARTIN COUNTY, INDIANA.

LaSALLE SPRING, MARTIN COUNTY, INDIANA.

	Cu. In. per U. S. Gallon.
Sodium sulphate.(Na$_2$SO$_4$)	3.512
Potassium sulphate (K$_2$SO$_4$)	.184
Aluminum sulphate (Al$_2$(SO$_4$)$_3$)	.056
Sodium chloride (NaCl)	1.440
Magnesium chloride (MgCl$_2$)	5.616
Silica (SiO$_2$)	.728
Total solids	126.328

	Cu. In.
Sulphuretted hydrogen	10.32

Free sulphur has coated white the rocks on each side of the rill, between the spring and the river. The water of the spring is very clear and sparkling with bubbles of escaping gas. It has a temperature of 56° F., and the output is about 75 gallons per minute. The taste is slightly bitter, but not enough so to be disagreeable. It is recommended in circulars sent out by the owner, Frank Brassine, as especially efficacious in diseases of the kidneys, such as diabetes, chronic inflammation, etc., also in dyspepsia and other stomach troubles.

IMPROVEMENTS.—A two-story frame hotel of 22 rooms, stands on a terrace of the river bluff, 50 feet above the spring. A bath house with four tubs is located on a level spot just above the spring. The scenery about is wild and picturesque. White River furnishes facilities for boating and good fishing, bass, white perch, catfish and crappies being plentiful. Game is said to be abundant in the proper season. There is need of better roads between the railway stations and the spring. If these were provided, the amount of patronage would increase, for it is a place well worthy of visitation.

ELLIOTT SPRINGS.

WATER = *Saline-chalybeate*.

LOCATION.—On the southeast quarter Section 10 (3 N., 3 W.), five miles east of Shoals, and three-quarters of a mile north of Willow Valley, the nearest station on the B. & O. S.-W. Railway.

ORIGIN AND CHARACTER OF THE WATER.—Four springs bubble up through a vein of fire-clay near the top of a high wooded slope. The flow from each is about two gallons per minute of an acidulous chalybeate water, with a bitter astringent taste. A partial analysis by Dr. Adolph Gehrman, 103 State Street, Chicago, showed the presence of the following:

Bases.	*Acid Radicals.*
Iron.	Sulphuric.
Calcium.	Nitric.
Magnesium.	Hydrochloric.
Sodium.	Phosphatic.
Aluminum (trace).	

Total solids present—241.3 grs. per U. S. gallon.

"The solids present are such as would indicate a purgative water, the sulphates of sodium, calcium and magnesium predominating."

Dr. T. B. Ritter, of Orleans, Indiana, the owner, states that the water is especially valuable for diseases of the mucous membranes; also for skin diseases, ulcers, etc. It can be kept bottled for a long time and not lose its cathartic and diuretic properties. It is shipped to some extent, bringing $5.00 per barrel, or 20 cents per gallon. There are no improvements. A limited number of visitors can find accommodations at the farm house on the land. A well near this farm house, 16 feet in depth, contains eight feet of water of the same character.

SHOALS ARTESIAN WELL.

WATER = *Saline-sulphuretted.*

LOCATION.—Just east of Shoals, the county seat of Martin County, a town of 750 population, situated on the B. & O. S.-W. Railway, 150 miles west of Cincinnati, and 191 east of St. Louis.

ORIGIN AND CHARACTER OF THE WATER.—This well was sunk in 1887 by a local company, to a depth of 960 feet in search of oil or gas. It lacked about 700 feet of reaching Trenton limestone, the main reservoir of those bitumens in Indiana. At 900 feet a vein of mineral water was struck which filled the bore and issues in a weak artesian flow. The rill escaping contains a thick sediment of the blackish flakes of iron sulphide. The odor of hydrogen sulphide, while strong, is not enough so to be disagreeable. The water is very saline in taste, and for use it should be diluted freely with pure water.

An analysis by Karl Langenbeck, of Cincinnati, Ohio, Professor of Chemistry in Miami Medical College, proved the presence of the following mineral salts:

ANALYSIS OF WATER FROM SHOALS ARTESIAN WELL.

	Grains per U. S. Gallon.
Silica (SiO_2)	2.7184
Alumina (Al_2O_3)	.6352
Sulphide of Iron (FeS)	1.3776
Sodium chloride (NaCl)	1303.4400
Potassium chloride (KCl)	47.3040

	Grains per U. S. Gallon.
Potassium nitrate (KNO₃)............................	7.8640
Lithium chloride (LiCl).............................	2.9352
Magnesium chloride (MgCl₂)........................	9.6832
Magnesium bromide (MgBr₂)........................	2.2376
Magnesium iodide (MgI₂)........................	.0040
Calcium sulphate (CaSO₄)..........................	203.0160
Calcium chloride (CaCl₂)............................	2.6512
Calcium carbonate (CaCO₃).........................	32.5256
Calcium sulphide (CaS).............................	24.4288
Calcium disulphide (CaS₂)...........................	18.8856
Calcium hyposulphite (CaS₂O₃)......................	133.0720
Ammonium chloride (NH₄Cl)........................	8.3480

Total solids...................................1801.2264

	Cu. In. per U. S. Gallon.
Sulphuretted hydrogen (H₂S)........................	32.4312
Carbonic acid gas (CO₂).............................	10.8584

"The water is strongly sulphurous in odor, and of a salty-alkaline-bitterish taste. It is faintly tinged greenish-yellow, by the contained bi-sulphide of calcium and has always a small black deposit of sulphide of iron. Protected from the atmosphere it keeps perfectly, remaining clear and unchanged in color. But if the containing bottle remain uncorked, the water becomes gradually of a deep greenish-yellow color, then becomes turbid, depositing white sulphur, while the supernatant water becomes clear and colorless. Ultimately all the sulphur disappears, through oxidation, the water containing the equivalents in sulphates and hyposulphites.

"It may be doubted if the water contains hyposulphite of lime as it issues from the earth. This may be purely a product of oxidation incident to the collection of the water in bottling. However this may be, this factor which is so important in the water, as analyzed, will always be present as an important factor, as the patient would get it. The analysis is, therefore, of the bottled water, of the product which interests the physician and not that of the water collected with extreme precautions to exclude atmospheric influence.

"The water instantly blues red litmus paper, showing its alkaline character, and turns a deep violet color on addition of sodium nitroprusside, showing that its sulphur is largely combined as sulphides. The presence of these is, from a chemical point of view, the most characteristic feature of the water."—*Langenbeck*.

The water from the Shoals well has been shipped extensively to customers in Louisville, Cincinnati and a number of the larger towns of southern Indiana. It is held in high esteem by the citizens of Shoals as an alterative and as a remedy in skin diseases, catarrh, etc.

MONROE COUNTY.

KETCHAM'S SULPHUR SPRING.

WATER = *Saline-sulphuretted.*

LOCATION.—In the northwest quarter of Section 7 (7 N., 1 W.), about three miles southwest of Smithville, a town on the C., I. & L. (Monon) Railway, 228 miles south of Chicago, 95 miles north of Louisville. A loop of the same railway runs within a short distance of the spring. The latter is distant seven and a half miles southwest of Bloomington, the county seat.

ORIGIN AND CHARACTER OF THE WATER.—A spring, flowing a small stream of water, wells up through a rift in the Harrodsburg limestone in the bed of Clear Creek. A cavity has been drilled in the limestone about the outlet of the spring, and a pump inserted which is reached by a raised platform. The water of the spring is heavier than that of the stream, and by means of the pump can be secured when the creek overflows the spring. No analysis of the water has been made. It has a strong odor of hydrogen sulphide and the bitter taste of that gas combined with sulphates, probably magnesium or sodium. It has been used with good effect locally for such diseases as are benefited by the common saline sulphuretted waters of this region of the State. The scenery about the spring is varied and picturesque, especially that along the bluffs of Clear Creek.

ORCHARD'S SULPHUR SPRING.

WATER = *Saline.*

LOCATION.—On the northwest quarter of Section 19 (8 N., 1 E.), about five miles southeast of Bloomington.

ORIGIN AND CHARACTER OF THE WATER.—A spring flowing about 20 gallons an hour, emerges from the base of a bluff of Knobstone shale. The water is strongly impregnated with sulphates derived by leaching through the shale, and for that reason has a very bitter taste. An analysis will probably show it to be quite like the Clark County mineral waters, which emerge from a similar shale. The water of some wells in the vicinity possess also a slight saline taste from the same source.

* * *

A third spring producing a saline-sulphuretted water, wells up in the bed of Salt Creek about a mile north of Guthrie and very near the Monroe-Lawrence county line. It is on the west side of the creek, about five feet from the bank and is covered during high water. A keg has been sunk about the orifice and the water, almost black with flakes of iron sulphide, presents a strong contrast to the muddy waters of Salt Creek, being plainly visible to passengers on the Monon Railway, which runs along the brink of the stream.

MONTGOMERY COUNTY.

VAN CLEVE'S SPRINGS.

WATER = *Alkaline-chalybeate.*

LOCATION. — Near the northern limits of Crawfordsville, the county seat, a city of 7,000 population, situated on the C., I. & L. (Monon); the Peoria Division of the Big Four and the Michigan Division of the Vandalia railways; 44 miles west of Indianapolis; 148 miles south of Chicago.

ORIGIN AND CHARACTER OF THE WATER.—A group of five springs, now owned and utilized by the Crawfordsville Water Company, issue from gravel at the base of a bluff 40 feet in height. Several six-inch driven wells, flowing water of the same character, have been sunk near the springs to a depth of 80 feet.

An analysis of the water of these springs made by Dr. Thad. M. Stevens, of Indianapolis, and published in the report of this Department for 1875, is as follows:

ANALYSIS OF WATER FROM VAN CLEVE'S SPRINGS, CRAWFORDSVILLE, INDIANA.

Potassium carbonate (K_2CO_3)	.144
Sodium carbonate (Na_2CO_3)	.168
Magnesium carbonate ($MgCO_3$)	3.824
Ferrous carbonate ($FeCO_3$)	.616
Calcium carbonate ($CaCO_3$)	9.800
Sodium chloride ($NaCl$)	.704
Sodium sulphate (Na_2SO_4)	.200
Magnesium sulphate ($MgSO_4$)	7.320
Silicic acid (H_4SiO_2)	.072
Total	22.848

"Carbonic acid and oxygen gases are held in solution, which render the water agreeable to the taste. The water acts as a laxative, febrifuge and tonic invigorator." It is very feebly mineralized and may be used freely. The iron will be found of service in anemic conditions. The water is collected in an impounding reservoir and from there pumped to a stand pipe.

GARLAND DELLS MINERAL SPRINGS.

WATER = *Neutral.*

LOCATION.—Among the breaks of Sugar Creek, 12 miles south-west of Crawfordsville and five miles northwest of Waveland, a station on the T. H. & L. and C. & S. E. railways, 38 miles north-east of Terre Haute. Marshall, a station on the C., I. & W. Railway, 56 miles west of Indianapolis, is four miles distant from Garland Dells. Carriages can be secured at either of these places for the springs. An electric railway from Crawfordsville to the springs is under contract and will probably be built in 1903.

ORIGIN AND CHARACTER OF THE WATER.—Three springs, about 100 feet apart, flow from crevices near the base of the Mansfield sandstone, on the south side of a deep ravine. The point of issue is about 125 feet below the crest of the hill on which the hotel is located, and 115 feet above the level of Sugar Creek in the valley below. The overflow of water from the springs finds its way into a stream called "Little Ranty," which, during the ages past, has eroded its way through the sandstone to its present level, thus forming the ravine.

The water of No. 1, the upper spring, is very clear, odorless and tasteless. A basin three and a half feet deep has been blasted out in the stone and then walled up. A gasoline engine is used to pump the water to a 30-barrel tank at the hotel.

Spring No. 2, the middle one, has not been improved. A portion of the water flows through an iron pipe, making it easier to obtain for drinking purposes.

The lower spring, No. 3, is likewise confined only in part. Its waters are said to be much more laxative than either of the others. A brownish red precipitate of iron oxide about the orifice, indicates a stronger chalybeate water than in the other springs.

Partial analyses of the waters made some years ago by Dr. J. N. Hurty, showed the presence of the following mineral salts per U. S. gallon:

ANALYSES OF WATERS FROM GARLAND DELLS, MONTGOMERY COUNTY, INDIANA.

	No. 1. Grains.	No. 2. Grains.	No. 3. Grains.
Calcium carbonate ($CaCO_3$)	12 to 16	12 to 16	12 to 16
Magnesium carbonate ($MgCO_3$)	10 to 15	8 to 12	10 to 12
Iron oxide (FeO)	trace	trace	trace
Sodium chloride (NaCl)	trace	1 to 2	1 to 2
Sodium sulphate (Na_2SO_4)	trace	trace	trace
Sodium carbonate (Na_2CO_3)	trace	trace	trace
Silica (SiO_2)	.....	.....	trace

Carbonic acid gas—small amount in each spring.

"The total amount of solid matter runs from 30 to 36 grains per gallon in each spring. The waters answer every test for purity and are unexceptionable as potable waters." The three springs flow about 60 gallons per minute, the amount showing but little depreciation in the dryest season.

IMPROVEMENTS.—Garland Dells, or "Shades of Death," has been open to the public as a resort for almost 20 years, and has been a camping ground for pioneers from the earliest settlement. In 1815 Government surveyors noted these springs as land marks on their records. At that time Indians in great numbers were using the high bluffs above the springs for their camping grounds.

About 1895, a company known as the Garland Dells Mineral Springs Association was organized, and secured control of 300 acres of land, including the springs. A 40-room frame hotel, eight cottages and numerous tents with board floors were erected. These furnish accommodations for almost 200 persons during the season, which lasts from May 1st to November 1st.

The scenery about the "Shades of Death" ranks among the most picturesque in the State. Professor Collett, in the report of this Department for 1875, thus describes some of the features of the place: "'Little Ranty,' flowing from the south, approaches in a flume-like passway, cut 50 feet deep in heavy sandstone, and thence rushes in a filmy sheet 45 feet down an almost perpendicular bank of dark shale, like an endless ribbon with warp of silver and woof of sparkling crystals. Silver Cascade is nestled away in an amphitheatre, 200 feet in diameter, crowded with shrubs, ferns and tenderest wild plants, here untrodden and unseen. Traveling ferns creep over and cling to the ragged masses of tufa, which guard the narrow entrance from the eye of the careless observer. More than a hundred feet above, tall oaks and pines, encircling the rim, swing their branches together across the cove and chasm." Here also grow the pine, yew, hemlock and cedar in abundance, while many rare forms of ferns, orchids and other herbaceous plants bring delight to the visiting botanist. Sugar Creek, flowing over its rocky bed, is a famous place for boating and bass fishing. Wherever the visitor may wander, among the hills and ravines along this portion of its course, new scenes of interest and of beauty will be presented. The scent of evergreens and all the spicy odors of the forest primeval will greet him, while a coolness peculiar to these shaded glens will, even in the hottest day of midsummer, invigorate and please. That these gifts of nature, together with the purity of the waters, are a panacea to the ailing, many will testify who in the past have visited this charming resort of Garland Dells.

*MORGAN COUNTY.

MARTINSVILLE MINERAL WELLS.

WATER = *Alkaline-saline-sulphuretted.*

LOCATION.—In different parts of Martinsville, the county seat, a city of 4,200 population, situated on the west fork of White River, 30 miles southwest of Indianapolis. The I. & V. Branch of the Pennsylvania Railway and the Indianapolis and Martinsville Electric Railway furnish easy access from Indianapolis. From Cincinnati and points east the city may be reached by the Fairland, Franklin and Martinsville Branch of the Big Four Railway.

Martinsville possesses all modern improvements of a city of its size. It lies at the foot of a range of varied and beautiful hills on the east and north, with White River winding toward the west and south through the valley below, thus providing most pleasing and romantic scenery. The streets are broad and clean, are lined on either side with spreading shade and forest trees, and lead out into smooth gravel-road drives which wind away among the scenic hills and valleys into the beautiful country beyond.

ORIGIN AND CHARACTER OF THE WATER.—Nine wells, sunk to depths ranging from 668 to 704 feet, produce a copious supply of alkaline-saline-sulphuretted water. Seven of these wells are connected with sanitariums which will be mentioned below; one is in Forest Grove Park, just west of the city, and the other is on the farm of C. S. Cunningham, one and a half miles south.

The first well was sunk in search for gas in 1887, to a depth of 1,470 feet. It was in the west part of the city, near the I. & V. Railway, on the grounds of the present site of the Barnard Sanitarium. In it, as in the other wells, the first vein of mineral water was struck at about 620 feet and a second vein at 640 to 650 feet. From 700 feet down the bore was wholly dry. The top of Trenton was reached at 1,700 feet.

After penetrating the drift, which is 90 to 117 feet in thickness, the wells at Martinsville pass through a formation of Knobstone shale 120 to 140 feet in thickness. Below this is about the same thickness of limestone which overlies 150 or more feet of black Genesee shale. The Corniferous and Niagara limestones are then entered, and the latter, at about 600 feet from the surface, becomes water bearing. The amount of water increases within the next 75 or 100 feet to its maximum flow. The rate of flow per minute, as determined in 1896 at several of the sanitariums, was as follows:

Home Lawn Sanitarium, 40 gallons; Highland Sanitarium, 25 gallons; Barnard's Sanitarium, 28 gallons; Martinsville Sanitarium, 35 gallons. Since then most of the wells have been closed in and connected with pumps, so that now only the one at Barnard's flows naturally.

The water at all the wells is clear and sparkling with carbonic acid and other gases. The odor of hydrogen sulphide is present, but not strong. The taste is agreeable, being but slightly bitter; a pinch of salt to the glassful renders it more palatable to many. The temperature, as it flows from the Barnard well, is 54° F.; at other points, after passing through pipes for some distance, it ranges from 56° to 60.°

Four analyses of the Martinsville water have been made, two by Dr. W. E. Stone, of Lafayette; one by Dr. J. N. Hurty, of Indianapolis, and one by Dr. T. C. Van Nuys, of Bloomington. These, reduced to the common standard of grains per U. S. gallon, are herewith printed side by side for comparison:

ANALYSES OF WATERS FROM MARTINSVILLE MINERAL WELLS.

	STONE. Martinsville Sanitarium Well.	STONE. Home Lawn Well.	HURTY. Forest Grove Park Well.	VAN NUYS. Barnard Well.
Sodium chloride (NaCl)	58.580	55.861	44.429	18.630
Potassium chloride (KCl)	1.775	14.779	1.559	20.485
Magnesium chloride (MgCl₂)	.....	.....	8.490	7.502
Calcium chloride (CaCl₂)	.....	.....	31.707	10.121
Sodium sulphate (Na₂SO₄)	1.879	1.697	.....	.....
Potassium sulphate (K₂SO₄)	.....	.....	.....	.897
Sodium sulphide (Na₂S)	.....	.....	.533	1.091
Calcium sulphide (CaS)	.....	.....	.500	.....
Potassium sulphide (K₂S)	.....	.....	.713	.....
Calcium carbonate (CaCO₃)	16.902	6.555	4.245	7.327
Magnesium carbonate (MgCO₃)	15.359	5.359	1.819	.....
Sodium carbonate (Na₂CO₃)	2.482	3.272	2.292	.....
Alumina (Al₂O₃)	.661	.997	.....	.....
Silica (SiO₂)	.556	8.456	.....	.....
Total solids	98.194	96.976	96.288	66.053

	Gases.			
	Cu. In.	Cu. In.	Cu. In.	Cu. In.
Carbon dioxide (CO₂)	21.24	45.50	47.980	23.07
Hydrogen sulphide (H₂S)	.86	6.92	20.725	1.02

In connection with the analysis furnished of the Forest Grove water, Dr. Hurty made the following statement: "This water will be found alterative, resolvent and antacid, and generally will be found gently aperient. Its richness in carbonic acid gas will make it gratifying and agreeable to the stomach, while the sulphuretted hydrogen will act as anti-ferment and eliminant. The proportion of sulphides of calcium, sodium and potassium in each pint seems particularly happy, as the quantities here shown are those in which they are most frequently given."

It will be seen that Drs. Stone and Hurty agree very closely as to the number of grains of solid matter contained in the water, but differ widely as to the forms of salts in which this solid matter occurs. This difference is, however, only the individual opinion of each chemist. The water of all the wells comes from the same level and the same vein, and the mineral constituents can, therefore, vary but little, if at all.

IMPROVEMENTS.—Soon after the water was first found at Martinsville, a bath house for utilizing it was opened up on a small scale by Mr. Barnard. This was just across the street from the well, and was burned after a year or two. A second and enlarged house was then erected on the present site. As the curative properties of the water became recognized and its fame spread, the guests increased largely in number and enterprising citizens began the erection of new and commodious sanitariums for their accommodation. The benefits to Martinsville from the finding of the water have been many. The city almost doubled in population between 1890 and 1900. Many new dwellings and business houses were erected and the place is now well known, not only in Indiana, but throughout the Union.

At present five sanitariums furnish treatment and home-like accommodations for thousands of patients throughout the year. These are as follows:

Martinsville Sanitarium and Mineral Springs Hotel.—This is a large two-story frame structure, located opposite the I. & V. Depot. The grounds and buildings occupy an entire block. The lawn between the sanitarium and the railway station is spacious and well shaded. There are 86 rooms for guests; 17 well-equipped bath rooms with facilities for mineral, vapor and electrical baths; billiard and pool rooms, offices, etc. The building is steam heated, electric lighted and in every way fitted up in modern style. The front, facing the shady lawn, is a delightful promenade and a most enjoyable resort, its entire length being brilliantly lighted by electric light, and in the winter season a space of 275 feet of it is enclosed in glass, thus permitting the guests who congregate there to experience the sensations of the warmth of summer in the midst of winter's inclement weather.

PLATE IX.

MARTINSVILLE SANITARIUM AND MINERAL SPRINGS HOTEL, MARTINSVILLE, INDIANA.

Two mineral wells furnish an inexhaustible supply of water which is piped to various drinking fountains and to all parts of the building. A resident physician of long experience devotes his entire time to looking after the needs of the patients.

Home Lawn Mineral Springs. — This sanitarium and hotel is located four blocks east of the public square and seven blocks southeast from the I. & V. Station, where free wagonettes meet all trains. The site is ten feet higher than the level of the I. & V. Railway and the wide lawn contains many large and beautiful trees. The sanitarium consists of three buildings, two brick and one frame, connected by wide enclosed, steam heated and electric lighted corridors. The south building contains the offices and bath rooms, the latter being ten in number, equipped with solid porcelain tubs and also with facilities for vapor, Russian and electric baths. A deep well furnishes a copious supply of the celebrated mineral water. The middle building of brick has been recently erected for hotel purposes. It and the north one contain 46 finely furnished apartments for guests, a number of them with private bath rooms attached. Billiard and music rooms furnish means of indoor amusement. The veranda in front, 130x20 feet in size, is enclosed completely with immense panels of plate glass and steam heated, thus forming a "winter sun parlor" which is much enjoyed by the patients during cold and damp weather. In the evening it is often used as a dancing pavilion or for private theatricals. The proprietors are experienced physicians who give the sanitarium their undivided attention.

Highland Hotel and Sanitarium.—Located five blocks northeast of the I. & V. Depot, on the brow of a hill 25 feet above the railway level. From its broad verandas a fine view is afforded of the surrounding valleys and undulating country beyond White River. The building is three stories in height and of modern construction and equipment. It contains 70 rooms for guests and ten bath rooms, all finely furnished. There are also facilities for electric, vapor and shower baths. Two large music and amusement rooms furnish a place for indoor recreation. One of these is supplied with billiard tables and gymnasium apparatus. From a deep well an unlimited supply of mineral water is piped to all parts of the building. The resident physician in charge has had long experience with the water and understands fully its curative powers for different diseases.

National Hotel and Sanitarium.—Located three squares southeast of the I. & V. Depot and one block west of the public square. This is a large two-story frame building, with wide veranda on the second floor, which furnishes a delightful promenade, 180 feet in length.

The hotel contains 25 rooms for guests, and ten well equipped bath rooms, each with separate cooling room at side. The ladies' bathing department is on the second floor, thus securing greater privacy. The building is heated throughout by steam, and possesses other modern impovements. An attendant physician is constantly at hand, and an adequate supply of mineral water is piped from a deep well on the grounds to all parts of the building.

Barnard Sanitarium.—This, the oldest bath house and sanitarium in the city, is located one block south of the I. & V. Depot. It is a two-story frame building used chiefly for bathing purposes. There are two deep wells on the grounds, one flowing a plentiful supply of mineral water. There are 28 bath rooms, well equipped for mineral, vapor and mud baths. An experienced physician is in regular attendance. The building is heated by steam, and there are sleeping accommodations for a limited number of guests, but most of the patients room and board elsewhere.

ORANGE COUNTY.

ORLEANS MINERAL WELLS.

WATER = *Saline* (?).

LOCATION.—Near the center of Orleans, a town of 1,300 population, situated on the C., I. & L. (Monon) Railway, 62 miles north of Louisville. The French Lick Springs Branch of the same railway joins the main line at the town.

ORIGIN AND CHARACTER OF THE WATER. — Two wells, formerly flowing, now pumped, one being located in a handsome grove one block north of the center of the town; the other two blocks southwest, at the northwest corner of the school house square. These wells were started for gas in 1889, but at a depth of 176 feet struck a strong vein of mineral water, which for several years flowed out of a three-inch casing, three feet above the surface. The casing was in time destroyed by the sulphuric acid in the water, and the flow ceased. Pumps were then inserted and are now used, the supply of water being seemingly inexhaustible. The water is clear and odorless, but has quite a bitter taste, probably due to the presence of Epsom and Glauber's salts. No analysis has been made. The temperature of the water as pumped is 55° F. It is used quite extensively by the citizens of Orleans as a laxative, and as a remedy in kidney troubles, and is deserving of more extended development than it has received in the past.

MOORE MINERAL WELL.

WATER = *Saline* (Purgative).

In the summer of 1902 a third well was sunk in the outskirts of Orleans, on property belonging to W. T. Moore. No data regarding the depth of the well is available, but a strong flow of mineral water resulted. An analysis of a sample of this by T. W. Smith, of Indianapolis, resulted as follows:

ANALYSIS OF WATER FROM MOORE MINERAL WELL, ORLEANS, INDIANA.

Bases and Acid Radicals.	*Grains per U. S. Gallon.*
Silica (SiO_2)	3.04
Ferrous oxide (FeO), Aluminum oxide (Al_2O_3)	1.05
Calcium (Ca)	19.18
Magnesium (Mg)	8.70
Sodium (Na)	18.59
Potassium (K)	3.72
Sulphate (SO_4)	113.76
Chlorine (Cl)	9.20
Total	177.24

The above constituents are probably combined as follows:

	Grains per U. S. Gallon.
Silica (SiO_2)	3.04
Iron and aluminum oxides ($Fe_2O_3+Al_2O_3$)	1.05
Calcium sulphate ($CaSO_4$)	67.13
Magnesium sulphate ($MgSO_4$)	43.50
Sodium sulphate (Na_2SO_4)	45.85
Sodium chloride (NaCl)	9.50
Potassium chloride (KCl)	7.10
Total solids	177.17

This water is similar to but not so strong as those described above from the springs issuing from the New Providence shales of Clark County, and it may be that it comes from the same formation. Taken in quantity, it will act as an active cathartic. In smaller doses it will be found remedial in stomach and liver troubles.

PAOLI ARTESIAN WELLS.

LOCATION.—Three wells, each producing an artesian flow of mineral water, are located within the environs of Paoli, the county seat, a town of 1,200 population, situated on the French Lick Branch of

7—Geol.

the Monon Railway, 10 miles distant from French Lick, and eight
miles from the main line of the Monon at Orleans.   Five trains run
daily each way between French Lick and Paoli.

(a) PAOLI LITHIA SPRING.

WATER = *Saline-sulphuretted.*

ORIGIN AND CHARACTER OF THE WATER.—The water of this so-
called spring comes from a well 1,000 feet in depth, which was sunk
on the north side of Lick Creek about one-quarter of a mile west of
the court house for gas or oil, in 1892.   A vein of mineral water
strongly charged with hydrogen sulphide, was struck at 250 feet,
while a second vein, containing lithia, was found in a blue shale at
1,000 feet.   The two veins were allowed to mix and at present flow
from an iron pipe into a stone basin at the rate of about two gallons
per minute.   An analysis of the water, made by Dr. W. A. Noyes, of
Terre Haute, showed the presence of the following mineral ingredients:

ANALYSIS OF WATER FROM PAOLI "LITHIA SPRING."

	Grains per U. S. Gallon.
Calcium sulphate (CaSO$_4$)	101.124
Magnesium chloride (MgCl$_2$)	4.395
Magnesium sulphate (MgSO$_4$)	52.138
Magnesium carbonate (MgCO$_3$)	20.430
Lithium bi-carbonate (LiHCO$_3$)	1.630
Sodium chloride (NaCl)	120.433
Potassium chloride (KCl)	2.364
Silica (SiO$_2$)	0.747
Alumina (Al$_2$O$_3$)	0.093
Ferrous carbonate (FeCO$_3$)	0.251
Total solids	308.605

Gases.	*Cu. In.*
Hydrogen sulphide (H$_2$S)	1.591
Free carbon dioxide (CO$_2$)	5.914

Besides the above, a trace of calcium phosphate and small amounts
of strontium sulphate, sodium bromide and sodium borate were
present.

This is one of the few deep wells of the State in which the water
is not excessively charged with common salt.   It has but a slight odor
of hydrogen sulphide, though bluish-black flakes of iron sulphide
are abundant in the stone receptacle.   The taste is a sweetish saline
and quite agreeable.   In the circulars sent out by the proprietors,

this water is advertised as being "unexcelled as an eliminator of diseased conditions of the system and as a blood purifier and remedy" for 38 named diseases. It is piped to the "Mineral Springs Hotel" near the center of the town, and is also shipped, bringing $2.50 per case of 24 quart bottles.

(b) Paoli Gas Well.

Water = Saline-sulphuretted.

ORIGIN AND CHARACTER OF THE WATER.—A well sunk for gas in 1897, developed a strong vein of mineral water in a hard limestone at a depth of 1,130 feet. Quite a quantity of gas issues with the water. The well is located in low ground, 122 yards east of the lithia well above described. The water rises just to the surface and the output is about five gallons per minute. It is quite salty in taste but not bitter, has a temperature of 58° F. and but a slight odor of sulphuretted hydrogen. An analysis make by Chas. B. Stout, a student at Earlham College, showed the mineral constituents of the water to be as follows:

ANALYSIS OF WATER FROM THE PAOLI GAS WELL.

	Grains per U. S. Gallon.
Magnesium sulphate ($MgSO_4$)	127.692
Magnesium chloride ($MgCl_2$)	149.434
Magnesium nitrate ($Mg(NO_3)_2$)	1.506
Calcium sulphate ($CaSO_4$)	10.369
Calcium chloride ($CaCl_2$)	185.337
Iron chloride ($FeCl_2$)	.231
Iron carbonate ($FeCO_3$)	2.669
Sodium silicate (Na_4SiO_4)	70.268
Sodium phosphate (Na_3PO_4)	4.300
Sodium chloride ($NaCl$)	614.537
Ammonium chloride (NH_4Cl)	4.757
Total solids	1171.100

(c) Paoli Sulphur Well.

Water = Saline-sulphuretted.

ORIGIN AND CHARACTER OF THE WATER.—This well was sunk to a depth of 250 feet, in 1895, in search of mineral water, as two wells, one put down by Studebaker Brothers, one-half mile west, and another on the John Maris farm, one mile east, had both developed veins of water strongly charged with hydrogen sulphide. The attempt was successful, a good vein of flowing water being found at

the depth mentioned. The well is located on the south bank of
Lick Creek, one-quarter of a mile east of the lithia well, and 400
feet south of the public square. A kiosk, or open building, has been
erected above the well. The water is quite bitter with the taste of
Epsom salt and hydrogen sulphide, and has a temperature of 56° F.
It is used at the Mineral Springs Hotel, and quite extensively by
the citizens of the town. The waters of both the lithia well and gas
well could be readily piped to the sulphur well and would there flow,
thus furnishing three waters, each possessing distinct medicinal virtues.

IMPROVEMENTS.—The Paoli Mineral Spring Hotel, a three-story
building of brick and stone, with accommodations for 100 guests,
and a number of well-equipped bath rooms, was erected for the express purpose of a resort and sanitarium, where the mineral waters
of Paoli could be used. Billiard halls, bowling alleys and ball rooms
afford means of indoor recreation. The scenery about Paoli is varied
and pleasing, and good roads diverging from the town furnish excellent opportunities for driving, cycling or walking.

LAMBDEN SULPHUR SPRING.

WATER = Saline-sulphuretted.

LOCATION.—On the land of Nathan Lambden, three-fourths of a
mile northeast of West Baden, on the south bank of Lost River.
The French Lick Branch of the Monon Railway runs just above the
spring. Postoffice, West Baden.

ORIGIN AND CHARACTER OF THE WATER.—A strong flowing spring
emerges from the base of the limestone bluff of Lost River, here 20
feet in height, and flows about 30 feet into the waters of that stream.
The output is about eight gallons per minute, of water which is dark
with particles of iron sulphide. The odor of sulphuretted hydrogen
is strong; the temperature 55° F., and the taste of the water very
similar to that of the Pluto Spring at French Lick. A frame building stands on the top of the bluff above the spring. It was built
a number of years ago and fitted up for bottling the water for shipment, but the enterprise was short-lived. Both in quantity and
quality the water is excellent, but the surroundings are not especially
favorable for a sanitarium.

RYAN AND MICKLER SPRINGS.

WATER = *Saline-sulphuretted.*

LOCATION.—These springs are about 100 feet apart, Ryan being in the southeast quarter of the northeast quarter, and Mickler in the northeast quarter of the northeast quarter of Section 10 (1 N., 2 W.), about one-half mile up French Lick Creek from the village of French Lick.

ORIGIN AND CHARACTER OF THE WATER.—Ryan Spring wells up in the bed of French Lick Creek, while Mickler is about 20 feet back from the bank of that creek. The latter is owned by Dr. J. L. Howard, of West Baden, who proposes developing it in the near future. The flow from both springs is rather small, but the water is of the same character as found at French Lick and West Baden.

RHODES' MINERAL SPRINGS.

WATER = *Saline-sulphuretted.*

LOCATION.—On the land of E. B. Rhodes, one-quarter of a mile southeast of the postoffice at West Baden.

ORIGIN AND CHARACTER OF THE WATER.—A spring wells up through a crevice in the Chester limestone. A wooden casing or box, five feet square and 12 feet deep, has been sunk above the outlet and is full of water. This is one of the oldest known springs in the valley of French Lick Creek, its waters being used by the early settlers years before the springs at West Baden, one-third of a mile northwest, were improved. The water is of the same character as that of the leading springs at French Lick and West Baden.

A bore was sunk by Mr. Rhodes about 30 rods northwest of this spring to a depth of 91 feet. The bore passed through 27 feet of surface material (soil and clay) and then through limestone to the bottom, where, in a soft, shaly limestone, a vein of sulphur water was developed, which flows above the surface. The overflow is carried through a ditch into a large cistern, and from this through a public ditch into Lost River. The water resembles closely that produced by the natural springs throughout the valley. It is Mr. Rhodes' intention to further improve both the well and spring and to erect a large hotel in the near future.

FRENCH LICK SPRINGS.

Water = *Saline-sulphuretted.*

Location.—In the west half of Section 3 (1 N., 2 W.), French Lick Township, Orange County, at the terminal of a branch of the C., I. & L. (Monon) Railway, 279 miles south of Chicago, 80 miles northwest of Louisville, 18 miles southwest of Orleans, where the branch railway connects with the main line of the Monon. Five trains run daily each way between Orleans and French Lick. Four trains also run daily between French Lick and Mitchell, where connection is made with the B. & O. S.-W. Railway for passengers from Cincinnati, St. Louis and intermediate points.

Origin and Character of the Water.—Three strong flowing mineral springs emerge from crevices in the Chester limestone at the point of junction of that formation with the overlying Mansfield sandstone. *Pluto Spring*—The largest and most noted of these is Pluto Spring, the water of which wells up from a perpendicular cleft in the limestone at the rate of about 18 gallons per minute. It has a constant temperature of 56½° F., a strong odor of sulphuretted hydrogen, and a bitter taste, due to the presence of large quantities of Epsom and Glauber's salts and other sulphates. Four analyses of the water of this spring have been made, one by Dr. J. G. Rogers, in 1869; a second by Prof. E. T. Cox, in 1870; a third by Mariner & Hoskins, of Chicago, in 1899, and the fourth at the Columbus Medical Laboratory, of Chicago, in 1901. The analyses made by Professor Cox and at the Columbus Medical Laboratory gave the percentage composition of the bases and acid radicals present as follows:

ANALYSES OF WATER FROM PLUTO SPRING, FRENCH LICK, INDIANA.

Bases and Acid Radicals.	COX. Parts per 1,000,000.	COLUMBUS MEDICAL LABORATORY.	COX. Grains per U. S. Gallon.*	COLUMBUS MEDICAL LABORATORY.
Lime	675.92	703.60	39.413	41.027
Soda	1140.20	1226.90	66.485	71.541
Potash	41.72	.....	2.433	.....
Magnesia	723.26	387.32	42.173	22.584
Alumina	48.10	trace	2.805	.....
Chlorine	1185.96	1065.00	69.153	62.100
Carbonic acid..............	690.55	266.02	40.266	15.511
Sulphuric acid..............	845.55	1631.00	49.304	95.104
Silicic acid.................	9.42	24.40	.549	1.423
Oxide of iron...............	1.90	trace	.111	.....
Total	5362.58	5304.24	312.692	309.290

*Reduced from grains per imperial gallon by multiplying by .833.

PLATE X.

PLUTO SPRING, AT FRENCH LICK, INDIANA.

The compounds of mineral salts present, according to the views of the different chemists, are as follows:

	ROGERS.	COX.	MARINER & HOSKINS.	COLUMBUS MEDICAL LABORATORY,
		Grains per U. S. Gallon.		
Calcium sulphate (CaSO₄)......	60.59	13.005	72.88	99.628
Potassium sulphate (K₂SO₄)....	.....	1.009	.....	.....
Sodium sulphate (Na₂SO₄)......	22.37	3.391	96.36	39.651
Magnesium sulphate (MgSO₄)...	18.12	55.652	.....	20.070
Aluminum sulphate (Al₂(SO₄)₃)..	trace	4.983	.....	.....
Calcium carbonate (CaCO₃).....	6.92	33.470	13.14	.....
Sodium carbonate (Na₂CO₃).....	.....	3.995	.....	.....
Potassium carbonate (K₂CO₃)...	.....	2.769	.....	.....
Magnesium carbonate (MgCO₃).	1.59	43.907	trace	32.573
Calcium chloride (CaCl₂).......	5.35	27.408	.....	.....
Sodium chloride (NaCl).........	140.54	118.197	33.28	116.328
Magnesium chloride (MgCl₂)....	.:...	4.246	56.88	.....
Silicic acid (SiO₂)..............	.....	.549	.....	1.423
Iron oxide (FeO)..............	trace	.111	.....	.....
Iodides and bromides..........	.....	trace	.....	.....
Undetermined matter..........	.54	.....	.....	.....
Total solids................	256.02	312.692	272.54	309.673
Gases.	*Cu. In.*	*Cu. In.*	*Cu. In.*	*Cu. In.*
Hydrogen sulphide (H₂S).......	25.05	5.595	5.40	5.233
Carbon dioxide (free) (CO₂).....	15.00	6.111	.....	.....

In an article in the Western Journal of Medicine for December, 1869, Dr. Joseph G. Rogers calls attention to these springs, after visiting them and making a careful quantitative analysis of the waters. The original analysis is given in the paper referred to, the amount of sulphuretted hydrogen being given as 25.05 cubic inches of gas in a wine gallon; that of carbonic acid gas as 15.00 cubic inches. The doctor first suggested the name "Pluto's Well," which was favorably received, and by which it has since been generally known.

It seems that in the various transcriptions which have been made of the analytical table of Dr. Rogers, the figures of his analysis above given have suffered a decided change, often some of them not appearing at all. The comparatively low figures for the amount of hydrogen sulphide gas in the tables given by the other chemists are due to the fact that their samples of water were not examined until some time after their arrival in the laboratory, after much of the gas had disappeared. Dr. Rogers' examinations were made at the well, and his figures regarding the gases are, therefore, to be accepted as correct.

The water of Pluto Spring has the widest reputation of any mineral water occurring in Indiana. It has been bottled and shipped for many years, and thousands of people have visited its source and have been benefited by the outing and the use of the water. It has been found beneficial in many cutaneous diseases and is valuable as a diuretic, alterative, laxative or saline aperient. It is especially adapted to persons who lead a sedentary life.

Bowles Spring.—This spring issues from the base of a sloping, wooded hillside, 320 yards northwest of Pluto. It wells out at the base of a mass of Mansfield sandstone, of which the hill is mainly composed. The output of the spring, in September, 1901, was about six gallons per minute, having a temperature of 56½° F. A white sulphur deposit coats objects close to the outlet; and the overflow is through a ditch containing much black iron sulphide. The water is quite bitter, and smells and tastes strongly of sulphuretted hydrogen. It is bottled and shipped, but not to a large extent.

An analysis of the water from Bowles Spring, made in the Columbus Medical Laboratory, Chicago, Ill., in 1901, resulted as follows:

ANALYSIS OF WATER FROM BOWLES SPRING, FRENCH LICK, INDIANA.

Bases and Acid Radicals.	Parts per 1,000,000.	Grains per U. S. Gallon.
Nitrogen	2.630	.....
Hydrogen sulphide.	23.720	.....
Silica	12.000	.700
Iron and alumina	1.000	.058
Calcium oxide	593.000	34.578
Magnesium oxide	321.440	18.743
Sodium oxide	989.000	57.669
Chlorine	810.580	47.265
Sulphuric anhydride	1421.000	82.859
Carbonic acid	237.500	13.849
Total	4411.870	255.721

The above constituents are probably combined as follows:

	Parts per 1,000,000.	Grains per U. S. Gallon.
Calcium sulphate (CaSO₄)	1440.14	83.974
Magnesium sulphate (MgSO₄)	316.59	18.460
Sodium sulphate (Na₂SO₄)	644.50	37.581
Magnesium carbonate (MgCO₃)	453.40	26.438
Sodium chloride (NaCl)	1518.41	88.539
Silica (SiO₂)	12.00	.700
Iron and alumina	1.00	.058
Total solids	4386.04	255.750

	Cu. In.
Hydrogen sulphide gas (H₂S)	3.667

PLATE XI.

INTERIOR OF PAGODA AT PLUTO SPRING, FRENCH LICK, INDIANA.

Plate XII.

At Fresh Water Spring, French Lick, Indiana.

Proserpine Spring.—Located 100 yards east of Pluto, in front of the newer portion of the hotel. The water rises just to the level of the floor of the large circular depression about the spring, which has been excavated and then cemented. The output is small, about five gallons per minute, of a more saline water than is afforded by the other two springs. The temperature is also higher, being $58\frac{1}{2}°$ F., while the odor and taste of sulphuretted hydrogen is milder. Two analyses of the water of this spring have been made, one in 1869, by Dr. J. G. Rogers, and a second in 1901, at the Columbus Medical Laboratory, Chicago. Only the latter gave a percentage composition of the bases and acid radicals, as follows:

ANALYSES OF WATER FROM PROSERPINE SPRING, FRENCH LICK, INDIANA.

Bases and Acid Radicals.	Parts per 1,000,000.	Grains per U. S. Gallon.
Nitrogen	3.50	.....
Hydrogen sulphide	26.98	.....
Silica	13.60	.793
Iron and alumina	trace	...,..
Calcium oxide	679.60	39.627
Magnesium oxide	369.28	21.532
Sodium oxide	1105.95	64.488
Chlorine	958.50	55.890
Sulphuric anhydride	1573.00	91.722
Carbonic acid	292.60	17.062
Total	5023.07	291.114

According to the views of the two chemists, the mineral compounds present in the water of Proserpine Spring are as follows:

	ROGERS.	COLUMBUS MEDICAL LABORATORY.
	Grains Per U. S. Gallon.	
Sodium carbonate (Na_2CO_3)	10.52	.....
Magnesium carbonate ($MgCO_3$)	4.50	29.598
Calcium carbonate ($CaCO_3$)	20.29	.....
Sodium sulphate (Na_2SO_4)	36.72	35.916
Magnesium sulphate ($MgSO_4$)	29.33	22.321
Calcium sulphate ($CaSO_4$)	141.00	96.235
Sodium chloride (NaCl)	90.92	104.696
Potassium chloride (KCl)	5.01	.....
Magnesium chloride (MgCl)	8.05	.....
Silica (SiO_2)	1.69	.793
Iron and aluminum carbonates	2.49	trace
Total solids	350.52	289.559
Gases.	*Cu. In.*	*Cu. In.*
Carbonic acid (CO_2)	10.116	.....
Sulphuretted hydrogen (H_2S)	17.000	4.103

With the analyses submitted by the Columbus Medical Laboratory of the waters from the three springs at French Lick was the following statement: "These waters were examined to determine the number of bacteria, the presence of disease-producing bacteria, bacterial evidence of sewage contamination, etc. There were no disease-producing bacteria, and no evidence of sewage contamination. The water was excellent from a sanitary standpoint.

"The waters are a carbonated, sulphuretted solution of sulphates, carbonates and chlorides of magnesium, sodium and calcium. In addition, there are traces of iron and aluminum, but these are in too small quantities to add value to the waters.

"After all, a great and perhaps the greatest advantage of a sojourn at the springs is drinking large quantities of good water, without reference to the salts and gases. Here one drinks very freely of a sanitary water, free from disease-producing bacteria, and, lastly, a great adjunct is the good air and the opportunity for exercise. A course of ten days to two weeks of these waters, together with outdoor exercise and moderate eating, is highly beneficial to every one, whether they are sick or not."

HISTORY* AND IMPROVEMENTS.—French Lick Springs are the oldest known springs of natural mineral water in Indiana. Their history long antedates the coming of the white man. The aboriginal inhabitants of the region were the Miamis and the Piankeshaws, but Indians from other tribes came here to drink the healing waters; the tract surrounding the springs being held as neutral ground on this account. The French of Vincennes were the first white settlers, being in quest of salt, and a salt depot was attempted by them, but was broken up by the hostility of the Indians in the latter part of the eighteenth century. The saline character of the water tempted the deer, buffalo and other animals of the forest, and from this fact it was known as a "lick;" hence the name "French Lick."

General George Rogers Clark, in the latter part of the eighteenth century, mentions this region in his memoirs of his famed expedition to Kaskaskia and Vincennes as a great resort for deer and buffalo. In 1832 the government sold a large tract of land, including both West Baden and French Lick Springs, to Dr. Wm. A. Bowles. About 1836 Dr. Bowles formed a partnership with one John Hungate. They opened a little store in French Lick village, and also put up a small frame hotel, for at this time people were beginning to flock here to partake of the health-giving water. In 1840 John A. Lane,

*For most of the facts relating to the History of French Lick and West Baden Springs, I am indebted to Dr. John L. Howard, of West Baden.

8—Geol.

PLATE XIII.

FRENCH LICK SPRINGS HOTEL, FRENCH LICK, INDIANA.

a traveling doctor, passed through the country and drank of the water. He saw at once the possibilities of the place, and secured a lease from Dr. Bowles for five years at $500 a year. The hotel was a plain frame building, standing at the foot of the hill on which had been erected the old French fort many years before. For a long period it could only be reached by stage from Orleans, Mitchell or Shoals, they being the nearest railroad stations.

In 1846 Dr. Bowles resumed the management, which he retained until 1864, when he rented the hotel and springs to Dr. Samuel Ryan for 15 years. Under Dr. Ryan's management a new impulse was given to the business, and much improvement was made. In 1880 the property was sold by the heirs of Dr. Bowles to a stock company, of which Dr. Ryan was the head. This company owned it until 1895, when it was purchased by some Louisville parties, who in turn sold it to the present proprietors in 1901, for $410,000. Of this amount $385,000 was paid for 400 acres of land surrounding the springs and the improvements thereon, and $25,000 for 80 acres adjoining, upon which several deep wells had been sunk, which threatened to diminish the flow of Pluto Spring. Four of these wells have been drilled within one-quarter of a mile of French Lick and three-quarters of a mile of West Baden, viz.: the Wells and Andrews well, in 1890; the Cerberus well, in 1897; the Baden-Lick and the H. E. Wells bores in 1901. These wells are all within a few hundred feet of each other, and veins of sulphur water were struck at 40, 200 and 480 feet from the surface. Only the deepest vein, however, resembled the output of the natural springs.

The fall of 1897 was marked by an extreme drouth, and after the Cerberus well had been drilled the French Lick Springs dropped three and one-half feet in their natural level, and lost a large percentage of their gaseous constituents. The Pluto Spring was especially affected, but as soon as the wells were plugged it regained, for the most part, its constant effervescence and boldness of flow.

The improvements at French Lick Springs are those of a first-class sanitarium and resort. They consist of a large hotel and two annexes, furnishing accommodations for 700 guests, and equipped with steam heat, electric lights, etc. A modern bath house is connected with the main hotel by a heated vestibule, and is fitted up with every facility for giving mineral, Turkish, Russian, electric, mud and other baths. The Casino contains the latest regulation bowling alleys, with all the modern improvements, new billiard and pool tables and gymnasium. A dancing pavilion, enclosed in glass and surrounded by galleries, is one of the largest in the country. For out-of-door exercise there are golf, tennis, croquet and baseball grounds. The park in front of the hotel contains many magnificent forest trees, as do also the wooded slopes of the hills which border this park on the west. Game is plentiful in the region about the springs. A large addition to the hotel has been recently completed, making these famous springs a resort the equal of any in the Union as a place for recreation and health recuperation.

WEST BADEN SPRINGS.

WATER = *Saline-sulphuretted.*

LOCATION.—One mile northeast of French Lick Springs, above described, in the north half of Section 34 (2 N., 2 W.), a short distance from the station of West Baden, on the French Lick Branch of the C., I. & L. (Monon) Railway. Postoffice, West Baden.

ORIGIN AND CHARACTER OF THE WATER.—A number of springs break forth from the Chester limestone, at the junction of that formation and the overlying Mansfield sandstone. Of these, four have been improved by excavating large circular basins, six to ten feet in depth, about their outlets and then cementing the floor and walls of these basins. By this means a natural flow above the level of the floor of the basin is obtained, as the flow of no one of the springs would reach the natural level of the surface of the low land of French Lick Creek, in which they are located. The springs are known respectively as Nos. 1, 3, 5 and 7.

No. 7 Spring.—Of these No. 7 is the principal one. Its basin is located near one side of the bottling works, to which its waters are in part pumped. When first improved, its basin was excavated 17 feet to a hard, flinty limestone or bed rock. A large curb was sunk about the outlet, and the regulation cement-lined basin then completed. The output of the spring in September, 1901, was about 12 gallons per minute, of clear, sparkling water, having a temperature of $56\frac{1}{2}°$ F., and possessing a strong odor of hydrogen sulphide and the characteristic bitter taste of the saline waters of this valley. An analysis of the water of this spring was made for this paper by Dr. W. A. Noyes, of Terre Haute, who reported on it as follows:

ANALYSIS OF WATER FROM NO. 7 SPRING, WEST BADEN, INDIANA.

Bases and Acid Radicals.	Parts to 1,000,000.	Grains per U. S. Gallon.
Silica	7.6	0.443
Calcium	577.2	33.671
Magnesium	228.2	13.312
Sodium	514.1	29.990

ANALYSIS OF NO. 7 SPRING—CONTINUED.

Bases and Acid Radicals.	Parts to 1,000,000.	Grains per U. S. Gallon.
Potassium	33.9	1.977
Chlorine	798.0	46.551
Sulphate (ion)	2046.0	119.353
Carbonate (ion)	179.9	10.494
Hydrogen sulphide	32.5	1.896
Total	4417.4	257.687

Besides the above, traces of each of the following elements were found: Alumina, iron, barium, strontium, lithium, bromine, iodine, phosphate (ion), borate (ion).

These bases and acid radicals may be considered as combined in the following manner:

	Parts to 1,000,000.	Grains per U. S. Gallon.
Silica (SiO_2)	7.6	0.443
Calcium sulphate ($CaSO_4$)	1962.5	114.482
Magnesium sulphate ($MgSO_4$)	781.3	45.577
Magnesium carbonate ($MgCO_3$)	251.9	14.694
Potassium chloride (KCl)	64.5	3.775
Sodium sulphate (Na_2SO_4)	52.6	3.075
Sodium chloride ($NaCl$)	1264.5	73.745
Total solids	4384.9	255.791
	Cu. In.	Cu. In.
Hydrogen sulphide gas (H_2S)	32.5	4.922

This analysis shows the water to belong to the saline-sulphuretted group, and to be very similar to that of the leading springs at French Lick. The water of No. 7 Spring has been the principal one served hot to the guests at West Baden for a number of years. It has also been extensively bottled and shipped. A new company, called the West Baden Springs Water Company, has been recently formed for the purpose of distributing the waters of this and the other springs more extensively. That from No. 7 will henceforth be sold under the name of "Baden Sprudel."

No. 5 Spring.—This spring is located northeast of the bicycle track and about 20 rods east of No. 7. The floor of the circular basin surrounding it is about six feet below the level of the surface. A handsome pavilion of modern design has been erected above this spring, as well as above No. 3. In 1901 the output of the spring was about six gallons per minute, of water which bore a close resemblance in temperature, odor and taste to that issuing from No. 7. An analysis of the water from this spring was made in 1870 by Prof. E. T. Cox, with the following result:

ANALYSIS OF WATER FROM NO. 5 SPRING, WEST BADEN, INDIANA.

Bases and Acid Radicals.	Parts per 1,000,000.	Grains per U. S. Gallon.
Lime	539.11	31.436
Soda	765.26	44.622
Potash	19.37	1.129
Magnesia	610.76	35.613
Alumina	43.50	2.536
Chlorine	779.26	45.439
Carbonic acid	675.21	39.371
Sulphuric acid	601.30	35.062
Silicic acid	7.50	.437
Oxide of iron	1.50	.087
Totals	4042.77	235.734

The above constituents are probably combined as follows:

	Parts per 1,000,000.	Grains per U. S. Gallon.
Calcium sulphate ($CaSO_4$)	191.70	11.178
Sodium sulphate (Na_2SO_4)	53.28	3.107
Potassium sulphate (K_2SO_4)	23.48	1.369
Magnesium sulphate ($MgSO_4$)	619.83	36.142
Aluminum sulphate ($Al_2(SO_4)_3$)	77.28	4.506
Calcium carbonate ($CaCO_3$)	709.43	41.367
Sodium carbonate (Na_2CO_3)	19.08	1.113
Potassium carbonate (K_2CO_3)	10.71	.625
Magnesium carbonate ($MgCO_3$)	671.48	39.154
Calcium chloride ($CaCl_2$)	124.78	7.276
Sodium chloride ($NaCl$)	1337.18	77.971
Magnesium chloride ($MgCl_2$)	195.54	11.402
Silicic acid (H_4SiO_4)	7.50	.437
Oxide of iron (FeO)	1.50	.087
Totals	4042.77	235.734

Gases.	Cu. In.
Carbonic acid (CO_2)	5.163
Hydrogen sulphide (H_2S)	4.941

"This water, judging from the analysis, possesses the same medicinal properties as that of the French Lick Springs, but it contains less free gases and a less quantity of solid constituents in a gallon, being a difference in degree rather than in quality."—*Cox.*

No. 3 Spring.—This spring wells up about 12 rods north of No. 7. Its flow is about the same as that of No. 5, and the water possesses the same properties. The floor of the basin is seven feet below the surrounding level.

PLATE XIV.

(a) Pagoda or Spring-house, No. 5 Spring, West Baden Springs.
(b) Interior of Pagoda, Spring No. 5, West Baden Springs.

An analysis of its water, made in 1899 by Mariner & Hoskins, of Chicago, showed the presence of the following mineral compounds:

ANALYSIS OF WATER FROM NO. 3 SPRING, WEST BADEN, INDIANA.

Grains per U. S. Gallon.

Calcium carbonate ($CaCO_3$)............................... 11.68
Magnesium carbonate ($MgCO_3$)........................... trace
Calcium sulphate ($CaSO_4$)................................ 96.88
Magnesium chloride ($MgCl_2$)............................. 52.96
Sodium chloride ($NaCl$)................................. 20.20
Sodium sulphate (Na_2SO_4).............................. 61.16
                                                        ———
Total solids...242.88

Cu. In.

Hydrogen sulphide gas (H_2S)........................... 4.491

It will be seen that the chemists agree closely as to the amount of mineral salts present in the waters of the three leading springs at West Baden, their results being as follows:

Total Solids.
Grains.

No. 7 Spring—Analyzed by Noyes 255.791
No. 5 Spring—Analyzed by Cox 235.734
No. 3 Spring—Analyzed by Mariner & Hoskins........ 242.88

However, their individual opinions, as to the kinds of salts present and percentage of each, vary widely, as will be noted by reference to the different analyses. There is little doubt but that the waters of the three springs have a common source and approximately the same chemical ingredients, and their medicinal actions are essentially alike.

Spring No. 1.—This spring is located about half way between No. 7 and the hotel, beneath the opera house and club rooms, these buildings having been constructed above its artificial basin. The outflow is smaller than that of any of the other three, about three gallons per minute in 1901. No analysis of the water has been made. It differs but little, if any, from that of the others, though it is claimed to be a stronger diuretic.

HISTORY AND IMPROVEMENTS.—The tract of land now including West Baden Springs was a part of that bought from the United States by Dr. Wm. A. Bowles in 1832. He sold 770 acres, including West Baden Springs, to Dr. John A. Lane in 1846. Dr. Lane erected a small hotel and gradually improved the surroundings. Hugh Wilkins controlled the place from 1864 to 1872, during which time the hotel was greatly enlarged and other substantial improvements made. In 1873 Dr. Lane again took charge and held it for 10 years, when he sold 667 acres, including the springs, for $23,000 to a company of Paoli and Salem citizens, two of whom, Messrs. E. B. Rhodes and L. W. Sinclair, in time became sole owners. By persistent advertising and improving they finally made the resort famous throughout the United States, and shortly before the fire which completely destroyed the hotel, were offered $1,000,000 for the property. This fire occurred in May, 1901. Mr. Rhodes soon after sold his share to Mr. Sinclair, who organized a stock company and contracted for a new brick and stone hotel, to cost $514,000. This was completed in the fall of 1902. The main portion of this hotel is six stories high and contains 600 rooms. A dome of steel and glass, 200 feet in diameter, covers a large rotunda in the center of the building. Each room is supplied with hot and cold water and other modern equipments.

Aside from the hotel, the improvements consist of a fine bath house, with facilities for giving all kinds of baths, and with a large natatorium attached. A gymnasium, equipped with all the paraphernalia of a modern athletic club, an opera house, billiard rooms and bowling alleys, furnish plenty of means for indoor exercise and amusement. A double-decked, covered bicycle and pony track, one-third of a mile in length, is an unique feature, furnishing, as it does, a place for cycle racing at all seasons, as well as a popular walk during inclement weather. Enclosed within the bicycle track is a base-ball diamond, while tennis courts and croquet grounds are found in various places.

The West Baden Springs occupy a natural amphitheater in the valley of French Lick Creek. The hills that rise above this valley to a height of 60 to 80 feet, form a half circle back of the springs and grounds about the hotel. The slopes of these hills, as well as a large portion of the grounds, are wooded with magnificent specimens of many kinds of native forest trees. For years these grounds have been under the care of a landscape gardener. Rough pathways cut along the hillsides have given place to smooth, graveled walks, winding in and out among the stately trees. Unsightly embankments have been transformed into walled-up terraces, intersected here and there with stone stairways, on either side of which are carved pieces of statuary and urns, from which spring variegated flowers. Broad driveways leading to various points of interest throughout the country surrounding, tell of months of patient labor in hauling sand, stone and gravel with which to form the roadbeds. The new hotel but adds lustre to the beauty of these surroundings, and West Baden Springs well merit the name which they have often

PLATE XV.

(a) The double-deck track and baseball grounds, West Baden Springs.
(b) Upper deck of half-mile bicycle track and promenade at West Baden Springs.

received—"The Carlsbad of America," although in chemical composition their waters differ widely from those of their European namesake.

LOST RIVER MINERAL SPRINGS.

WATER = *Saline-sulphuretted.*

LOCATION.—Along Lost River, between Orangeville, a village situated in the northwestern part of Orange County, and West Baden.

ORIGIN AND CHARACTER OF THE WATER.—Several mineral springs well up from the bed, or issue from the bases of the bluffs of Lost River. One of these, one mile south of Orangeville, on land owned by the Travelers' Insurance Company, south half of Section 7 (2 N., 1 W.), is in the bed of the stream, and is covered during high water. A barrel has been sunk around the orifice of the spring, and a constant stream of water, highly charged with hydrogen sulphide, overflows. No analysis of the water has been made, but its taste, odor, etc., show it to be of the same character as that of the French Lick Springs.

Wilson's Spring is located about two miles southwest of the one above described, on the west half of the southwest quarter of Section 14 (2 N., 2 W.). It is one and a half miles north of West Baden, and is owned by John H. Wilson, County Surveyor of Orange County. The spring emerges from the base of a bluff on the bank of Lost River, and has an output of about four gallons per minute. The water is very similar to that at West Baden. Another spring of the same nature is on the farm of John A. Stackhouse, adjoining that of Mr. Wilson; while a third issues a little farther down the stream on the land of Chambers Campbell.

FLAT LICK SPRINGS.

WATER = *Saline-sulphuretted.*

LOCATION.—On the land of Thomas Lane, west half of Section 26 (1 N., 2 W.), two miles west of Helix, a postoffice six miles southwest of Paoli and five miles southeast of French Lick, the nearest railway station.

ORIGIN AND CHARACTER OF THE WATER.—Two springs emerge from crevices in a hard white limestone near the banks of Flat Lick Creek, a tributary of French Lick Creek. The large one flows four and a half gallons per minute, and the smaller about one-half as much, of a very clear, saline water, containing much sulphuretted hydrogen. No analyses of the waters have been made. They have been used locally for stomach and kidney troubles and are of the same nature as those at French Lick.

OWEN COUNTY.

SPENCER ARTESIAN WELLS.

WATER = *Saline-sulphuretted.*

LOCATION.—Two wells yielding an artesian flow of mineral water have been put down in Spencer, and a third about one-half mile northeast of the city. Spencer, the county seat, is a city of 2,100 population, situated on White River, 53 miles southwest of Indianapolis. The I. & V. Railway passes through the city while the C., I. & L. (Monon) connects with the I. & V. at Gosport, six miles east.

The streets are broad, beautiful, shaded avenues, forming cool, delightful walks and drives, frequently terminating in shady country roads, winding among the hills, through some of the wildest and most romantic scenery of the State.

ORIGIN AND CHARACTER OF THE WATER.—The first of the wells is located three squares north of the court house, near the high school building. It was sunk in 1889 to a depth of 1,150 feet. The mineral water was found in the Niagara limestone. The head of the water was sufficient to cause it to rise 65 feet above the well mouth, or 625 feet above tide. In 1890, after the well had been drilled 100 feet deeper, the estimated flow was 200 gallons per minute.

An analysis of the water, made by Dr. J. N. Hurty, of Indianapolis, revealed the presence of the following mineral salts:

ANALYSIS OF WATER FROM SPENCER ARTESIAN WELL.

	Grains per U. S. Gallon.
Calcium sulphide (CaS)	.393
Potassium sulphide (K_2S)	1.906
Sodium sulphide (Na_2S)	.940
Calcium carbonate ($CaCO_3$)	12.222
Magnesium carbonate ($MgCO_3$)	2.386
Sodium carbonate (Na_2CO_3)	4.162
Calcium chloride ($CaCl_2$)	8.110
Potassium chloride (KCl)	18.113
Sodium chloride (NaCl)	66.813
Magnesium chloride ($MgCl_2$)	5.031
Silica (SiO_2)	.360
Ferric oxide (Fe_2O_3)	.553
Alumina (Al_2O_3)	.713
Total solids	121.702

Gases.	*Cu. In.*
Hydrogen sulphide (H_2S)	1.796
Carbon dioxide (CO_2)	11.294

In September, 1901, the water, after flowing a square underground and emerging at a fountain at the corner of the high school yard, had a temperature of 64° F. The taste was an agreeable saline-sulphur. The odor of hydrogen sulphide was not strong.

A second well, sunk in the court house yard, at a level of 20 feet below that of No. 1, found the same water at 1,150 feet. The pressure of the outflowing stream is 62 pounds per square inch, and the output 350 barrels per hour, having a temperature of 66° F. The water from this well is used for drinking purposes, at three fountains in the court house yard, for street sprinkling purposes, etc. It is also supplied to the Central Sanitarium and Hotel.

The third well, put down on the farm of Calvin Fletcher, developed a smaller flow of the same water at a depth of 1,300 feet. It is not now utilized.

IMPROVEMENTS.—A large sanitarium and bath house was erected near the first well, at a cost of $20,000, and was in operation from 1890 to 1897. It was well patronized, having at times 100 or more patients. A change of ownership, and resulting change of parties in charge, caused dissatisfaction, litigation, etc., until the place was abandoned. It is now uninhabited and in a bad condition. If repaired and taken in charge by a good physician, it could, without much doubt, be made a paying institution, as the water is well worthy a more extended medicinal use than it is now receiving.

The "Central Mineral Springs Sanitarium and Hotel" is located on the east side of the public square, within one block of the railway station. It contains 24 rooms for guests and a well-fitted bath house, with facilities for mineral, vapor, Russian, shower and needle baths. The mineral water is piped from the well in the court house yard. Both hotel and bath rooms are steam-heated and are open to guests the year around.

GOSPORT ARTESIAN WELL.

WATER=*Saline-sulphuretted* (?).

LOCATION.—Within one block of the railway station at Gosport, a town of 750 population, located on White River, at the crossing of the I. & V. and C., I. & L. (Monon) railways, 44 miles southwest of Indianapolis, 204 miles southeast of Chicago, and 119 miles northwest of Louisville.

ORIGIN AND CHARACTER OF THE WATER.—A well 936 feet in depth was, in the autumn of 1895, bored by a citizens' stock company in the valley of a small tributary of White River, near the eastern side of the town. The well is cased about 500 feet to shut out salt water. A strong flow of "white sulphur" water was struck near the bottom of the bore, presumably in Niagara limestone. This water will flow freely at the top of a pipe 30 feet above the mouth of the well, or 610 feet above tide. In October, 1901, the flow was about 20 gallons per minute. As it issues from the discharge pipe it is quite clear, but becomes milky almost instantly, on account of the escaping bubbles of gaseous hydrogen sulphide and the resulting deposition of free sulphur. The water has the odor and taste of similar sulphur waters, but does not contain as much sodium chloride (common salt) as many of them. Its temperature is 63½° F. No analysis of the water has been made. It is quite similar, however, to the mineral waters at Martinsville and Spencer, and its medicinal effects are practically the same.

The stock company which sunk the well gave it to a smaller company of citizens on condition that a sanitarium and bath house be erected. This was done at a cost of $6,800, and was in successful operation until November, 1901, when it was destroyed by fire. The owners have not yet decided whether it will be rebuilt or not.

PARKE COUNTY.

MONTEZUMA ARTESIAN WELL.

WATER = *Saline-sulphuretted.*

LOCATION.—On the east bank of the Wabash River, in the southern part of Montezuma, a town of 1,200 population, situated on the C., I. & W. Railway, 67 miles west of Indianapolis; and within two miles of Hillsdale, a station on the C. & E. I. Railway, 155 miles south of Chicago and 23 miles north of Terre Haute. Also within one and a half miles of the C., I. & W. Crossing, a station on the Brazil Division of the C. & E. I. Railway.

ORIGIN AND CHARACTER OF THE WATER.—The bore producing the water was sunk in 1889, in search of gas, to a depth of 1,686 feet. It is located on a tract of nine and one-half acres of land abutting the channel of the Wabash River and about 30 feet above low water mark. At a depth of 298 feet in the bore a small vein of salt water was struck, and another at 450 feet, both of which had sufficient head to rise to the surface. At 1,200 feet, in a limestone immediately below the Devonian shales, the present flow of mineral water was developed. In a test it was shown that the water would rise in and overflow from a one and one-half-inch pipe 80 feet above the well opening, or 573 feet above tide.

An analysis of the water by Dr. W. A. Noyes, of Terre Haute, showed the mineral constituents to be as follows:

ANALYSIS OF WATER FROM THE MONTEZUMA ARTESIAN WELL.

	Grains per U. S. Gallon.
Calcium chloride	11.655
Calcium sulphide	3.553
Calcium sulphate	7.117
Calcium bi-carbonate	11.183
Magnesium chloride	9.975
Magnesium bi-carbonate	17.885
Potassium chloride	2.683
Sodium chloride	357.710
Silica	0.828
Alumina	0.070
Total solids	422.659

	Cu. In.
Hydrogen sulphide gas (H_2S)	9.678

In addition to the above, traces of strontium sulphate, calcium phosphate, lithium chloride, sodium bromide, sodium iodide and borax were present.

The flow of water has diminished little, if any, since the well was completed. In August, 1901, it was estimated at 17,000 barrels per day, or about 472 gallons per minute. The odor of hydrogen sulphide in the vicinity of the well is strong, but the taste, modified by the sodium chloride and other salts, is rather agreeable, and becomes more so by use. The temperature of the issuing water is 72° F. It is useful for catarrh, rheumatism, skin diseases and all other ailments for which mineral waters of a similar kind are used.

IMPROVEMENTS.—In 1890 a large frame hotel and sanitarium was erected on the grounds. A swimming pool 132x72 feet in size, nine feet deep at one end and gradually sloping to two and a half feet at the other, was excavated and lined with cement. Bath houses were built along one side of the pool. A steam-heated bath house, with 35 tubs, was also erected for use by invalids and when the water of the pool was too cool. The sanitarium was run successfully for several years, but dissensions finally arose between the proprietor and the citizens of Montezuma, and these, with a failure to properly advertise, caused the closing of the sanitarium. It is now used as a tenement house, and is in poor repair. The entire property was sold in 1900 to the present owner, Mr. G. W. Hughes, of Hume, Illinois, for $3,000.

The pool is still much frequented during the summer months. A charge of 25 cents is made for each bath therein, which includes the rental of bathing suit. During the month of July, 1901, the revenue from this source was $156.00.

The water is shipped to all who request it, but the demand is not as great as during the time the sanitarium was open. It brings $1.00 per barrel, or 10 cents per gallon on board the cars. This does not include the cost of receptacle. To the citizens of Montezuma it is free, and a large local use is made of it.

PIKE COUNTY.

COATES' SPRINGS.

WATER = *Alkaline-saline-chalybeate.*

LOCATION.—On the land of S. S. Shannon, southeast quarter Section 10 (1 S., 9 W.), eight miles southwest of Petersburg, the county seat, on the E. & I. Railway; eight miles northwest of Oakland City, on the St. Louis Division of the Southern Railway; 15 miles northeast of Princeton. Carriages or other conveyance may be obtained at these towns at reasonable rates. Postoffice, Coates' Springs. Daily mail.

ORIGIN AND CHARACTER OF THE WATER.—Three springs are found on the grounds. The one whose waters are most noted is located a few rods from the hotel, on the side of a gentle slope. The water is in a well-like basin, which has been excavated in sandstone rock. A section from the surface to the bottom of the spring is as follows:

	Ft.	*In.*
(1) Soil and yellow clay..................	4	..
(2) Sandstone	2	6
(3) Black sheety bituminous shale.........	0	4
(4) Sandstone	?	

A cavity two and a half feet in depth has been cut in the lower sandstone, which holds the water. The latter is drawn to the surface, as needed, in a bucket. It probably derives most of its mineral constituents by leaching through the black shale, which is rich in pyrites of iron and alumina.

These springs were formerly known as the West Saratoga Springs. The only analysis of the water available was under that name in Peale's "Mineral Waters of the United States."* It is accredited to E. T. Cox, and gives only the percentage of bases and acid radicals present, as follows:

---

*Bulletin 32, U. S. Geological Survey, 1886, p. 140.

ANALYSIS OF WATER FROM COATES' SPRING.

Bases.	Grains per U. S. Gallon.
Calcium oxide	2.024
Sodium and potassium	.142
Ferric oxide	1.874
Alumina	.183
Acid Radicals.	
Chlorine	1.040
Sulphuric acid	7.289
Phosphoric acid	.533
Insoluble matter	.466
Total solids	13.560

This combination of bases and acid radicals denotes that the principal salts present are iron sulphate, aluminum sulphate and calcium carbonate. The presence of the first two is clearly indicated by the taste, which is quite bitter and astringent. The water is clear and has a temperature of 64° F. It is said "to be very beneficial in malarial troubles; also in inflammatory rheumatism. When taken in quantity it usually acts as a purgative. Being especially strong in sulphates and iron, it should be taken only on the advice of a physician." It is shipped, when desired, at a rate of 10 cents per gallon. The same price is charged when taken away from the premises.

A second spring issues from a hillside about 100 yards southeast of the one above described. Its water has been piped some distance and issues in a stone basin arranged as a receptacle. No analysis was available. Judging from the taste, it contains only iron and calcium carbonates, and is, therefore, an ordinary chalybeate water. Its temperature is 63° F., and the flow about three gallons per minute.

A third spring, a short distance north of the hotel, possesses also a chalybeate water of less strength. The waters of both these minor springs are valuable chiefly as a diuretic, and in cases of anæmia, or poverty of the blood.

HISTORY AND IMPROVEMENTS.—Coates' Springs were first opened to the public in 1867 by the Hon. James A. Coates, then owner. They were under control of the present proprietor, S. S. Shannon, from 1871 to 1885, and gained quite a renown, being much frequented by citizens of Evansville, Vincennes and other places in southwestern Indiana. The farm was then leased to other parties, who gave little attention to the mineral waters. In 1900 they were again opened as a resort. The hotel has accommodations for 40 guests. There are good bowling alleys, croquet grounds, dancing pavilions, etc., while the spacious lawns and good country roads furnish excellent facilities for riding and driving. Many campers and picnic parties visit the place and partake of the waters. The hotel is open from May to November, though guests will be taken at any season.

SWEET SULPHUR SPRINGS.

WATER = *Alkaline-saline-sulphuretted.*

LOCATION.—Two miles north of Velpen, a station on the St. Louis Division of the Southern Railway, 84 miles west of Louisville; 189 miles east of St. Louis, and 57 miles northeast of Evansville. The railway makes a rate of one and one-third fare round trip for visitors to the springs during the season. Conveyances from the springs meet all day trains. They also meet night trains when notified in advance.

ORIGIN AND CHARACTER OF THE WATER.—Three springs issue about 100 feet apart from the base of a gentle slope, which rises to the west, 30 feet above their level. In Spring No. 1 the water rises in a stone basin one foot above the surface, and the flow is about four gallons per minute. In Spring No. 2 it does not flow, but is pumped. In No. 3 it flows, but only about one and one-half gallons per minute.

Analyses of the water from each of the springs have been made by L. D. Kastenbine, Professor of Chemistry, Louisville Medical College, who reported the presence of the following mineral salts:

ANALYSES OF WATERS FROM THE SWEET SULPHUR SPRINGS, PIKE COUNTY, INDIANA.

	Grains per U. S. Gallon.		
	No. 1.	*No. 2.*	*No. 3.*
Calcium sulphate ($CaSO_4$).........	47.159	18.136	38.952
Magnesium sulphate ($MgSO_4$).....	32.165	42.054	27.558
Calcium carbonate ($CaCO_3$).......	25.617	28.347	32.521
Magnesium carbonate ($MgCO_3$)....	2.821	2.154	.....
Ferrous carbonate ($FeCO_3$)........	.....	1.924	2.110
Sodium chloride ($NaCl$)..........	2.498	1.693	3.847
Potassium chloride (KCl).........	0.107	0.303	0.971
Silica (SiO_2).....................	0.091	0.876	0.752
Alumina (Al_2O_3).................	.015	0.126	.011
Total solids..................110.473		95.613	106.722
Gases.	*No. 1.*	*No. 2.*	*No. 3.*
Carbonic acid (cu. in.)............	4.843	5.987	4.197
Hydrogen sulphide (cu. in.).......	1.386	.....	1.911

The temperature of the waters in September, 1901, was 63° F., 63½° F. and 68° F., respectively. The taste of all is quite similar, being a bitter sulphur. The odor of hydrogen sulphide is present in all, though probably a little stronger in No. 3. The water will be found a good remedy in excessive acidity of the stomach on account of the small amount of sodium chloride and fair amounts of sulphates and carbonates. It is served hot, when desired, in a small building located near the springs.

IMPROVEMENTS.—A frame hotel, with accommodations for 80 guests, stands on the high ground west of the springs. The water is pumped by a gasoline engine into tanks, thence into the bath house, where it is heated. There are six well equipped bath rooms. A bowling alley, pool and billiard room, croquet grounds, dancing hall, etc., furnish facilities for amusement and exercise. A very pretty grove of native forest trees occupies a portion of the lowland to the east. The property belongs to the heirs of Charles Fisher, the former proprietor, who died a few years ago. It is now run under the management of Edward Fisher, 712 Twenty-third Street, Louisville, Kentucky. The hotel is open to guests from June 1st to October 1st. The majority of the visitors are from Louisville, St. Louis, Evansville and other points on the "Air Line" Railway.

* * *

Besides the springs above described, the following are mentioned by Dr. John Collett, in his paper on the "Geology of Pike County."* The time at our disposal would not allow of their visitation.

" 'Miller's Ague Spring,' Section 5 (1 S., 6 W.), is locally known as a 'cure' for that disease. The waters are a saline chalybeate, flowing out of ferruginous beds of sandstone. Their qualities are highly esteemed by those who have tried them.

" 'Milburn's Spring,' T. C. Milburn, proprietor, situated on the southeast quarter Section 35 (1 S., 7 W.), has a high reputation in that vicinity as a remedy for diseases of the stomach, bowels, kidneys and of the skin. It is generally known as the 'ague cure,' but is reputed as still more efficacious in derangements of the liver and digestive organs. Many certificates from reputable persons indicate especial virtue in cases of gravel and rheumatism. At the time of my visit, not less than 20 persons were drinking the water, and it was being hauled away so extensively as to almost exhaust the receiving cask. It contains salts of soda, magnesia and iron, with traces of bromine and arsenic. The spring flows out at about the level of coal K, the shales and roof stones of which are near by."

---

*Geological Survey of Indiana, 1872, pp. 265, 286.

PORTER COUNTY.

PORTER ARTESIAN WELL.

WATER = *Saline-sulphuretted.*

LOCATION.—On the grounds of the Chicago Hydraulic Press Brick Company at Porter, a town at the junction of the Lake Shore and Michigan Southern, Michigan Central and E., J. & I. railways, 40 miles east of Chicago and 12 miles southeast of Michigan City.

ORIGIN AND CHARACTER OF THE WATER.—This well was bored in search of gas to a depth of 860 feet. At present it flows about 60 gallons per minute of water that is highly charged with hydrogen sulphide, as well as with the following mineral salts:

ANALYSIS OF WATER FROM THE PORTER ARTESIAN WELL.

Grains per U. S. Gallon.

Sodium chloride ($NaCl$)	208.76
Calcium chloride ($CaCl_2$)	51.93
Magnesium chloride ($MgCl_2$)	38.71
Ammonium chloride (NH_4Cl)	0.44
Potassium chloride (KCl)	13.18
Potassium sulphate (K_2SO_4)	17.08
Calcium carbonate ($CaCO_3$)	11.14
Silica (SiO_2)	1.10
Total solids	342.34

This analysis was made by Dr. J. H. Salisbury, Professor of Chemistry in the Women's Medical College, Northwestern University, who speaks of the water as follows: "The water from Porter is very free from injurious organic matters. It is very useful for drinking at the well in cases which need alterative or laxative treatment, and is also useful for baths and for sanitarium purposes. Its sulphuretted hydrogen will not be long retained if exposed to the air."

* * *

The Blair artesian well is also located in the northwestern corner of Porter County. It is, however, so near to Michigan City that its waters have been described on a previous page under the head of Laporte County.

PLATE XVI.

WINAMAC ARTESIAN MINERAL WELL, WINAMAC, PULASKI COUNTY, INDIANA.

PULASKI COUNTY.

WINAMAC ARTESIAN WELL.

Water = *Saline-sulphuretted.*

LOCATION.—On the west bank of the Tippecanoe River, two squares northeast of the court house at Winamac, a town of 1,700 population, situated on the P., C., C. & St. L. Railway, 92 miles southeast of Chicago and 103 miles northwest of Indianapolis.

ORIGIN AND CHARACTER OF THE WATER.—The well producing the artesian flow was sunk by a citizens' stock company in 1889, to a depth of 1,260 feet. The vein of mineral water was developed in a limestone, 205 feet below the surface. When the bore was found to be devoid of gas it was plugged just below the vein of water, and the latter then rose about four feet above the surface of the terrace or second bottom of the Tippecanoe, on which the well is situated. This terrace is about 12 feet lower than the level of the city to the westward.

In October, 1901, the water was flowing at the rate of 20 gallons per minute. It was very clear and had a slight odor of hydrogen sulphide, which issues in sufficient quantity to keep the stone basin into which the water falls from the discharge pipes coated white with free sulphur.

A partial analysis of the water, made in the laboratory of the School of Mines of the University of Missouri, resulted as follows:

Bases.	*Grains per U. S. Gallon.*
Iron oxide	.082
Alumina	1.056
Magnesium	2.622
Calcium	.395
Sodium	2.339
Potassium	3.215

Acid Radicals.

Sulphates—large amount.
Chlorides—small amount.
Carbonates—medium amount.
Nitrates—trace.

The total solids are said to approximate 500 parts in 1,000,000. The water issues with a temperature of $53\frac{1}{2}°$ F. It has the slightly bitter taste of magnesium sulphate and kindred salts. Small quantities are shipped from time to time to parties in Indianapolis, Chicago and Crown Point, who are much pleased with its beneficial action in kidney and liver troubles. It is also said to be especially useful in dissolving uric acid crystals by diluting the urine.

The well is situated directly opposite a wooded tract on the east bank of the Tippecanoe, which is utilized as a private park, but which could be secured for sanitarium purposes. The river offers exceptional advantages for boating and fishing.

MUDGE ARTESIAN WELL.

WATER=*Alkaline-sulphuretted.*

LOCATION.—On the land of E. T. Mudge, southeast quarter Section 30 (31 N., 4 W.), Pulaski County, Indiana; two miles northwest of Medaryville, a station on the Michigan City Division of the C., I. & L. (Monon) Railway, 65 miles southeast of Chicago. The railway passes one mile east of the well.

ORIGIN AND CHARACTER OF THE WATER.—A well sunk for oil in the spring of 1902, passed through 70 feet of drift material, composed of sand, gravel and clay, then through 25 feet of black Genesee shale, and developed in the underlying Corniferous limestone, at a depth of 109 feet, a strong vein of mineral water. This water rose with such force above the surface that it put a stop to farther drilling, and the flow has continued unabated at the rate of about 40 gallons per minute.

An analysis of the water made by Dr. W. A. Noyes, of Terre Haute, resulted as follows:

ANALYSIS OF WATER FROM THE MUDGE ARTESIAN WELL, PULASKI CO., INDIANA.

Bases and Acid Radicals.	*Grains per U. S. Gallon.*
Silica (SiO_2)	0.560
Alumina (Al_2O_3)	0.099
Ferrous oxide (FeO_2)	0.011
Calcium (Ca)	2.648
Magnesium (Mg)	1.202
Potassium (K)	2.683
Sodium (Na)	3.943
Chlorine (Cl)	3.290
Sulphate (SO_4)	0.280
Carbonate (CO_3)	7.688
Hydrogen sulphide (H_2S)	1.277
Total	23.681

The above constituents may be considered as combined as follows:

Grains per U. S. Gallon.

Silica (SiO₂).. 0.560
Alumina (Al₂O₃).. 0.099
Ferrous carbonate (FeCO₃)............................ 0.023
Calcium carbonate (CaCO₃)........................... 4.731
Magnesium carbonate (MgCO₃)....................... 2.526
Potassium carbonate (K₂CO)......................... 4.363
Potassium sulphate (K₂SO₄) 0.507
Sodium chloride (NaCl)................................ 5.419
Sodium carbonate (Na₂CO₃)........................... 4.176

Total 22.404
Hydrogen sulphide gas (H₂S), 3.31 cu. in. per U. S. gallon.

Besides the above there were present in the water traces of titanium oxide, strontium sulphate, lithium carbonate, sodium phosphate, and sodium borate. The water is alkaline and contains a high amount of potassium in proportion to the sodium.

As it issues from the well it is clear and sparkling, with a slight but distinct odor of hydrogen sulphide. The well is much frequented by residents of the vicinity, who speak highly of the exhilarating or stimulating effects of its water. It will be found useful for bathing purposes, skin diseases and as an aperient. The well is situated on the north edge of a natural grove, which will furnish a delightful site for a sanitarium.

PUTNAM COUNTY.

McLEAN'S SPRINGS.

WATER = Alkaline-chalybeate.

LOCATION.—One and a fourth miles southwest of the court house at Greencastle, the county seat, a city of 3,700 population, situated 39 miles west of Indianapolis, 178 miles south of Chicago, and 145 miles north of Louisville, on the T. H. & I. (Vandalia), St. Louis Division of the Big Four and C., I. & L. (Monon) railways.

ORIGIN AND CHARACTER OF THE WATER.—Four springs, flowing about two gallons a minute each, issue a few rods apart from crevices at the junction of the Mansfield sandstone and the underlying subcarboniferous limestone, on the east half Section 29 (14 N., 4 W.). The springs are in a fine grove of native timber, which is much frequented by picnic parties. This grove is along the south side of the Vandalia Railway, one-half mile west of the city station on that line, and about the same distance northeast of Limedale, the junction of the Monon and Vandalia railways. The springs have been named the

"Daggy," "McLean," "Diamond" and "Dewdrop." The waters from the Daggy and Dewdrop springs were analyzed by Prof. E. T. Cox, and the results published in the report of this department for 1870, pp. 121-124:

ANALYSES OF WATERS FROM "DAGGY" AND "DEWDROP" SPRINGS, NEAR GREENCASTLE. INDIANA.

	Daggy.	Dewdrop.
Ferrous carbonate (FeCO$_2$)...................	.398	2.381
Calcium carbonate (CaCO$_3$)...................	14.148	11.883
Sodium carbonate (Na$_2$CO$_3$)...................	.090	.071
Potassium carbonate (K$_2$CO$_3$)................	.087	.074
Magnesium carbonate (MgCO$_3$)..............	4.700	5.335
Sodium sulphate (Na$_2$SO$_4$).....................	.133	.099
Magnesium sulphate (MgSO$_4$)................	1.050	1.036
Sodium chloride (NaCl)......................	.793	.695
Silica (SiO$_2$).............................	.087	.004
Alumina (Al$_2$O$_3$)............................	.157	.074
Loss and undetermined......................	.093	.228
Total solids...........................	22.157	21.884
	Cu. In.	Cu. In.
Carbonic acid gas (free)...................	3.005	2.98

"When fresh from the springs the water sparkles with the surcharge of carbonic acid gas and is cool and pleasant to the taste The temperature of the Daggy Spring is 56° F.; that of the Dewdrop, 52° F. The water of the Diamond Spring partakes of the character of the other two. It has a temperature of 51° F. at the fountain head; is alkaline to test-paper after standing a short time, and contains 21.0 grains of solid constituents in a U. S. gallon."

For a number of years the water of these springs was bottled and shipped to various points. Through a lack of advertising the demand gradually diminished and the shipment was finally abandoned. The purity and the character of the water and the pleasing natural surroundings merit a more extended use, and would justify the erection of a large hotel and sanitarium, which would doubtless soon become a popular resort for invalids and those who seek a healthful and cool retreat from the cares of business during the summer months.

MAHAN'S SPRING.

WATER = *Chalybeate.*

LOCATION.—On the northwest quarter Section 28 (14 N., 4 W.), about one-half mile east of McLean's Springs, described above, and one-quarter of a mile south of the Vandalia Railway station at Greencastle.

ORIGIN AND CHARACTER OF THE WATER.—This spring formerly issued as a seep, but a basin was dug out and otherwise improved a few years ago, and the water was then bottled and delivered to residents of Greencastle at a fixed price. The water is not sold at present but the spring is much frequented by residents and students. A large deposit of iron oxide from the water has been formed in and below the spring and the taste of this oxide is plainly perceptible in the water. The flow approximates 100 gallons per hour.

REELSVILLE ARTESIAN WELL.

WATER = *Saline-sulphuretted.*

LOCATION.—On the east side of the village of Reelsville, a station on the T. H. & I. (Vandalia) Railway, 47 miles west of Indianapolis, and 26 miles east of Terre Haute.

ORIGIN AND CHARACTER OF THE WATER.—This well, which for a number of years produced a fine artesian flow of mineral water, is situated on the west bank of the Walnut fork of Eel River, 18 feet above low water mark. It was sunk for oil about 1865. At a depth of 1,240 feet, in a hard cherty limestone, there resulted a strong flow of white sulphur water highly charged with sulphuretted hydrogen gas, and containing chlorides of sodium, calcium and magnesium; also sulphites of the same bases with traces of bromine and iodine. It had a pleasant saline, sulphurous taste and pungent odor, and was found to have great medicinal efficacy in cases of dyspepsia, rheumatism and ague.

During the historic "flood" of August, 1875, the overflow from the river washed sand and gravel into the bore and stopped to a large extent the flow. The water continued to ooze out until 1898, when some schoolboys placed rocks in the pipe and stopped the flow entirely. It could be readily opened if so desired.

SNOWDEN SPRINGS.

WATERS = *Alkaline-sulphuretted, and Chalybeate.*

LOCATION.—On the land of James Van Hook, northwest quarter of northeast quarter of Section 6 (15 N., 3 W.), about two miles northeast of Bainbridge, a town of 450 population, situated on the C., I. & L. (Monon) Railway, 170 miles southeast of Chicago. Roachdale, a station at the crossing of the Monon and C., I. & W. railways, 35 miles west of Indianapolis, is six miles north of the springs.

ORIGIN AND CHARACTER OF THE WATER.—Four springs issue from clefts in the Riverside sandstone, on the sides of a ravine. This ravine is 30 to 40 feet in depth and at the point where the springs issue only the same in width. It has been cut through the sandstone by a stream which has its source in these springs and others farther up, and which now flows in a sinuous course over the rocky bottom of the ravine, for a quarter of a mile or more, when it empties into Big Walnut Creek, one of the best bass fishing streams in the State.

At the point where the springs issue the sides of the bluff are precipitous and bend in a curve toward the northwest. A "white sulphur" spring, flowing two gallons per minute of clear sparkling water, issues on the west side, just below the bend and ten feet above the bottom of the ravine. The odor and taste of hydrogen sulphide is noticeable but slight. Enough is present, however, to coat with free sulphur some of the objects near the point of issue. On December 30, 1901, the temperature of the water was 47° F.; that of the air being 41° F.

Directly across from this spring, on the east side of the ravine, 35 feet distant and a foot or two higher, a second spring of crystal chalybeate water issues from another cleft. A basin has been cut out in the stone ledge at the point of emergence and the water overflowing from this falls down the side of the ravine, coating everything with a heavy deposit of brownish-yellow oxide of iron. The output of this spring, on the date mentioned, was about two gallons per minute, having a temperature of 48° F.

On the north side of the ravine, at the point of the bend, and about 40 feet distant from the springs above mentioned, the third and fourth springs issue from a long crevice, and flow over a ledge of sandstone into the stream below. These springs are but three feet apart, yet their waters are different in character and of a different temperature, that of the west spring being a "black sulphur" water, with a temperature of 45° F., while the eastern spring produces a

PLATE XVII.

b

d

VIEWS IN THE VICINITY OF SNOWDEN'S SPRINGS.

(a)   Starr's Falls, one-third mile south of the springs.
(b)   The White Sulphur spring.
(c) and (d)   Two views in the ravine in which the springs are located.

strong chalybeate water, with a temperature of 48° F. It is probable that the temperature of all of these springs varies three or four degrees during the year. That of the "black sulphur" water, in Spring No. 3, was the coldest water tested in the State.

The region within a mile or two of these springs contains some of the wildest and most picturesque scenery of central Indiana. Less than half a mile to the northeast is the "devil's backbone," a long ledge of rock, in places less than three feet in width, and with precipitous sides, dropping down 60 or more feet to the depths below. Here is one of the few spots in Indiana where the hemlock, *Tsuga canadensis* (L.), grows in its natural state, while the American yew, *Taxus minor* (Michx.), trails over the rocky sides of the gulch and flourishes in the deep, cool shade of its more majestic relative.

Other scenes of interest abound in the vicinity; while the nearness of Big Walnut Creek furnishes excellent fishing and boating facilities. Taking into consideration the quantity, quality and variety of the waters at Snowden's Springs, and the beauty of their natural surroundings, no better site for the erection of a large sanitarium and summer resort exists in Indiana.

ROACHDALE MINERAL SPRING.

WATER=*Chalybeate.*

LOCATION.—On the land of Albert Couck, one-third of a mile southwest of the center of Roachdale, a town of 1,000 population, situated at the crossing of the C., I. & L. (Monon) and the C., I. & W. railways, 35 miles west of Indianapolis, and 162 miles southeast of Chicago.

ORIGIN AND CHARACTER OF THE WATER.—A spring wells up in a low spot in a blue grass pasture, with a flow of about two gallons per minute. An excavation three feet in depth and walled with brick contains the water, which is clear and odorless, but has the characteristic taste of iron carbonate, and a heavy yellowish brown deposit of the same about the side of the rill bearing away the overflow. No analysis of the water has been made. Its temperature is 50° F., and it is much used by a number of the citizens of the town, who claim for it superior medicinal virtues.

* * *

A number of other chalybeate springs occur throughout the county, the waters of which are used locally. Among the most important of these are several springs just south of Brick Chapel, in Section 29 (15 N., 4 W.). Their water is similar in taste and appearance to that of McLean's Springs at Greencastle.

At Brick Chapel there is a well 25 feet deep, near the store; one 120 feet deep at the school house, and a third 140 feet deep at the cemetery, all of which furnish strong chalybeate water similar to that in the springs just south of the village. The water is used locally for household purposes. The two deep wells are reported to have penetrated 25 feet through glacial drift into and through a limestone and "flinty rock" into a soft blue rock which is probably the Knobstone.

RIPLEY COUNTY.

JOHNSON MINERAL SPRING.

WATER = *Chalybeate.*

LOCATION.—Three miles southeast of Versailles, on the land of Chas. Johnson, northwest quarter of the southeast quarter of Section 20 (7 N., 12 E.). Milan, the nearest railway station, is distant seven miles northeast from the spring. It is on the B. & O. S.-W. Railway, 42 miles northwest of Cincinnati.

ORIGIN AND CHARACTER OF THE WATER.—This spring, the only one of its character in the southeastern part of the State, emerges from the base of a mass of glacial drift which rises 30 feet above the level of the surrounding region. The flow at the surface is weak, but this is caused, in part at least, by the soaking away of the water in the loose soil. The flow could be largely increased by piping the outlet and conveying all the water into one receptacle. That the water is heavily charged with iron is shown by the large reddish-brown deposit of iron carbonate along the stream flowing from the spring. Its waters are now used locally, but for a long time were believed to be poisonous to both man and beast.

RUSH COUNTY.

CLARK ARTESIAN WELL.

WATER = *Saline.*

LOCATION.—One mile southeast of Carthage, a town of 1,100 population, situated on the Michigan Division of the Big·Four Railway, 37 miles east of Indianapolis.

ORIGIN AND CHARACTER OF THE WATER.—This well was bored for gas in 1888 to a depth of 860 feet. It produced quite a quantity of gas, and at the same time a large flow of mineral water, until 1898, when the gas supply became exhausted. The water still flows and is much used locally for affections of the kidneys. An analysis by Prof. J. W. Shepherd, of Terre Haute, Indiana, showed its mineral constituents to be as follows:

ANALYSIS OF WATER FROM CLARK ARTESIAN WELL, NEAR CARTHAGE, INDIANA.

	Grains per U. S. Gallon.
Sodium chloride (NaCl)	4101.2
Calcium chloride (CaCl$_2$)	2188.94
Alumina (Al$_2$O$_3$)	413.0
Magnesium chloride (MgCl$_2$)	208.2
Ferrous carbonate (FeCO$_3$)	30.85
Potassium chloride (KCl)	19.42
Calcium sulphate (CaSO$_4$)	15.88
Calcium carbonate (CaCO$_3$)	1.89
Total solids	6974.38

This water is remarkable chiefly on account of the large amount of chlorines and chlorides it contains.

* * *

A number of flowing wells have been sunk in the western part of the city of Rushville, the county seat, which yield a chalybeate water of good quality. The source of this water is a fine white sand. This is overlain with an impervious bed of blue clay called "hard pan," 14 to 15 feet in thickness. Above the blue clay are six to eight feet of soil, yellow clay and gravel. In the words of Dr. M. N. Elrod, "These artesian chalybeate wells of West Rushville are curious examples of subterranean streams or sheets of mineral water, held down by the impervious blue clay. The wells are dug in the usual manner, or dug a few feet and then bored through the clay. The water is found in the fine gravel or white sand overlying the bed rock. Pump logs were placed in some of the wells and tamped with clay until the water was forced to flow through the log. The quantity of water discharged was never great, and additional wells seemed to weaken the flow of those previously dug, indicating that the water probably comes from a compact saturated bed of sand that slowly gives up its superabundant moisture."

SHELBY COUNTY.

SHELBYVILLE MINERAL WELL.

WATER = *Alkaline-saline-sulphuretted.*

LOCATION.—Near the junction of the Big Four and Cambridge City branch of the P., C., C. & St. L. railways in the southeastern part of Shelbyville, a city of 7,500 population, situated 27 miles southeast of Indianapolis, and 84 miles northwest of Cincinnati.

ORIGIN AND CHARACTER OF THE WATER.—This well, which produces the "Shelbyville Lithia Water," was sunk in June, 1901, to a depth of 1,450 feet. The top of Trenton limestone was reached at 825 feet, and the bore is said to have penetrated the full thickness of that formation, the bottom being found at 1,415 feet. Below the Trenton, according to Mr. Jno. D. Pugh, who furnished me the data, a blue and more porous rock was found. This was undoubtedly the St. Peter's sandstone, a very porous formation well adapted for transmitting water, and the common source of much of the water in many of the deep artesian borings of northern Illinois and Indiana.

Ten feet in this sandstone a "white sulphur" water was encountered and 15 feet below this the vein of lithia water. The two veins mingled and arose in the bore to within 140 feet of the surface. An analysis of the water was made by Dr. J. N. Hurty, of Indianapolis, who reported the presence of the following mineral ingredients:

ANALYSIS OF WATER FROM SHELBYVILLE MINERAL WELL.

	Grains per U. S. Gallon.
Sodium chloride (NaCl)	696.570
Potassium chloride (KCl)	6.021
Lithium chloride (LiCl)	12.060
Sodium sulphate (Na_2SO_4)	48.190
Magnesium carbonate ($MgCO_3$)	45.762
Calcium carbonate ($CaCO_3$)	65.100
Alumina (Al_2O_3)	0.860
Iron oxide (Fe_2O_3)	0.297
Total solids	874.860

	Cu. In. per Gallon
Free hydrogen sulphide	1.78

"This is an antacid, anti-fermentative water, slightly laxative, and contains lithium and a small amount of iron. It will be found curative in stomach and bowel troubles and indigestion; and will also be found slightly laxative, and on account of the lithium it contains and also its great organic purity, it will cure rheumatism and various bladder disorders. The iron, which most probably exists as ferrous carbonate, is an important ingredient. It will also be found excellent for salt water baths."—*Hurty.*

In November, 1901, the water as it was pumped from the well to the bath rooms equipped by the owner, had a temperature of 51° F. As it emerges from the well it is quite dark with flakes of iron sulphide. After standing in the receiving tank these settle and the water is then clear, with a sweetish and quite strong saline taste. The odor of hydrogen sulphide is not sufficient to render it disagreeable. The water is shipped to order at 25 cents per single gallon, or $5.00 per barrel.

IMPROVEMENTS.—At the well only a pumping station has been erected to lift and force the water to the bath rooms described below and to the sanitarium of Dr. T. C. Kennedy, where it is used. This sanitarium is a private institution, complete with all modern conveniences. The rooms are large and cheerful, steam heated and well ventilated. Each patient is under the personal supervision of trained nurses at all hours.

The "Shelbyville Lithia Water Bath Rooms" were fitted up during the summer of 1901 by the owner of the well, Mrs. E. F. Hamilton, and her manager, Mr. John D. Pugh. The bath rooms are located in a three-story brick building on East Washington Street, near the public square. On the lower floor are the reception room, office, five bath rooms for gentlemen, cooling room, toilet rooms, rooms for vapor, shower and Turkish baths, etc. On the second floor are the bath rooms for ladies, with accompanying parlor, cooling room, etc. The equipment throughout is very fine, the tubs being of solid porcelain, the floors of tile or hard wood, with the other furnishings to match. In the basement are boiler and engine for steam heating, dynamos for electric lighting, water tanks, etc. About $12,000 have been expended in fitting up the interior of the building in good style, and the enterprise certainly merits a good patronage. Hotel accommodations at the bath house are as yet unprovided for, but excellent accommodations at reasonable rates can be secured at the different hotels and at many of the private residences of the city.

* * *

THERMAL WELLS.

Two thermal wells, or wells producing water above 75° F., have, in the past, been discovered in Shelby County. The following information regarding them was written by Dr. John Collett and published in the report of this department for 1881, page 68:

10—Geol.

"It is a well known fact that at the level of perpetual spring water a constant temperature of 52° F. is maintained in this latitude; thence downward, the temperature becomes higher with regular increments, and in this State the rate of increase has been found to be 1° F. for each space of 79 feet of depth. By this law we may, without estimating the cooling effects of the stony walls of the fissure and the inflow of surface water, safely conclude that a change of 28° F. indicates the source of supply at a depth of 2,212 feet.

"The Shelbyville thermal well was put down in December, 1870, in the eastern part of the city, near Little Blue River Bridge. At a depth of 18 feet the water was found to be warm, and at the bottom, 24 feet from the surface, a constant temperature, winter and summer, of 76° was maintained.

"The Barlow thermal well is near Barlow's Mills, Section 3 (13 N., 6 E.), nearly four miles west of Shelbyville. An old well, twenty-three feet deep, at the residence of Henry Barlow, had been used for household purposes and was favorably known for furnishing cold water, 52° F. Suddenly the water became warm, and was no longer desirable; the thermometer indicating 65° F. A pipe was driven in November, 1870, from the bottom, through fine sand and pebbles, resting in a bed of gravel, to a depth of 16 feet, or 39 feet from the surface. The water was found to have a temperature of 80° F., and during the next winter attained a maximum heat of 86°. These wells were excavated for potable water only, and being unfit for this use, were neglected and allowed to be filled up. If found permanent, these springs will invite the attention of those needing hot baths, and suggest that it would be cheaper (and surely more efficacious) to use the thermal waters of Shelby County, than the distant hot springs of southern regions."

TIPPECANOE COUNTY.

LAFAYETTE ARTESIAN WELL.

WATER == *Saline-sulphuretted-carbonated.*

LOCATION.—At the northeast corner of the court house square in Lafayette, a city of 18,500 population, located 63 miles northwest of Indianapolis on the Chicago Division of the Big Four Railway. The C., I. & L. (Monon), L. E. & W., and Wabash railways also pass through the city.

ORIGIN AND CHARACTER OF THE WATER.—The "white sulphur water" of the Lafayette artesian well had, for years, a reputation as great as that of any other mineral water in the State. The well was sunk in 1857-'58 to a depth of 230 feet. Its surface is 55 feet above low water mark in the Wabash River, or 560 feet above tide. The material passed through by the bore was as follows:

SECTION OF BORE OF LAFAYETTE ARTESIAN WELL.

		Ft.	In.
(1)	Drift composed of soil, clay, gravel and sand	170	0
(2)	Shales, blue and gray	28	6
(3)	Limestone—Corniferous (?)	11	6
(4)	Limestone—Niagara	20	0
	Total	230	0

The mineral water was struck in the Niagara limestone, 13½ feet above the bottom of the well. The flow of the water for some time was variable, ranging from nothing up to 275 gallons per hour. It finally settled down to a steady flow of about 200 gallons per hour. In 1895 this flow began to fail and finally stopped altogether. The county commissioners had the hole drilled a little deeper and then shot with a small quantity of nitroglycerin. This shattered the limestone to such an extent that the supply of water was wholly stopped. A new bore was sunk 40 feet northwest of the old, in 1900, to a depth of 231 feet. In this the water rose only to within 25 feet of the surface. It was pumped and a plentiful supply obtained as long as the pump was in good order, but the sulphuric acid in the water destroyed the iron tubing very rapidly. In August, 1901, the water was not being used, on account of a lack of pumping facilities, but a new pump with clay or wood tubing was soon to be put in.

An analysis of the water was made soon after it was first discovered, by Dr. Chas. M. Wetherill, who also prepared an extended report upon the well itself and the physical properties of the water. From this report I quote as follows: "The Lafayette artesian water is of an extreme limpidity when freshly taken from the well. The deposit upon the pebbles over which it flows is white, entitling it to the name of "white sulphur water." Standing in imperfectly closed vessels, a similar bluish-white deposit takes place. Under certain conditions, the deposit contains black flakes of sulphuret of iron. The smell of the water is strongly of sulphuretted hydrogen, so as to be perceived at a distance (with the wind) of two squares from the well. The taste is similar to that of the celebrated Kentucky Blue Lick water, though less strong. It is pleasantly brackish, resembling in taste the liquor from oysters freshly opened. The temperature of the water when first taken from the well is 56° F. Its density is 1.00523."

ANALYSIS OF WATER FROM ORIGINAL LAFAYETTE ARTESIAN WELL.

Grains per U. S. Gallon.

Calcium carbonate (CaCO₃)............................ 12.024
Magnesium carbonate (MgCO₃)....................... .400
Calcium sulphate (CaSO₄)............................ 56.016
Calcium chloride (CaCl₂)............................ 3.720
Magnesium chloride (MgCl₂)......................... 29.656
Sodium chloride (NaCl)................................ 324.768
Peroxide of iron with alumina, phosphate of lime, fluor-
     ide of calcium and faint trace of manganese...... .496
Silica .... .464

    Total...427.544

Gases.   *Cu. In.*
Hydrogen sulphide................................... 2.2960
Carbonic acid.......................................12.2024
Nitrogen 4.9280

By comparison Dr. Wetherill found that the water of the Lafayette artesian well contained "as much calcium carbonate as the water of the White Sulphur Springs, of Virginia; as much calcium sulphate as the same springs, and as the Sharon Sulphur and the Avon Lower Springs, of New York; as much magnesium chloride as the Blue Lick Spring, of Kentucky, and more iron and less silica than the same spring. One and a half gallons of the Lafayette artesian water contains as much common salt as one gallon of the Blue Lick water."

PAPER MILL ARTESIAN WELL.

WATER=*Saline-sulphuretted* (?).

LOCATION.—One and one-half miles south of the court house at Lafayette, near the junction of the C., I. & L. and L. E. & W. railways.

ORIGIN AND CHARACTER OF THE WATER.—A well was put down for gas in 1888 to a depth of 1,300 feet, a few rods south of the old paper mill and on the grounds belonging to the owners of that mill. A strong vein of "white sulphur" water was developed at a depth of 330 feet. In August, 1901, it was flowing at the rate of 15 gallons per minute. The water has an agreeable sweetish-saline taste combined with the odor and taste of hydrogen sulphide. No analysis has been made. Within five feet of the top of the bore, a spring of fresh water was issuing from the base of a gravel bluff, with an output of eight gallons per minute.

The sulphur water has for some time been jugged and delivered to many of the citizens of Lafayette. Large quantities of the water are also carried away by the nearby residents. It is regarded as a specific for some skin diseases; also for certain forms of indigestion.

The flow is sufficient and the quality of the water seemingly high enough to warrant the erection of a bath house and sanitarium for its more extended use.

BUCK CREEK ARTESIAN WELL.

WATER = *Saline-sulphuretted* (?).

LOCATION.—On the farm of S. T. Blood, one and one-half miles northwest of Buck Creek, a station eight miles northeast of Lafayette, on the Wabash Railway.

ORIGIN AND CHARACTER OF THE WATER.—The well producing this water was sunk for gas to a depth of 960 feet. At 600 feet a vein of mineral water was developed, which has since been flowing. In August, 1901, the output was about two gallons per minute of water which gives off a strong odor of hydrogen sulphide. A heavy deposit of the black flakes of sulphuret of iron is left in the stream bearing away the overflow from the well. The water is used locally as a laxative, for skin diseases, etc.

BATTLE GROUND SPRING.

WATER = *Chalybeate.*

LOCATION.—On the bank of Burnett's Creek, near the Tippecanoe Battle Ground, seven miles north of Lafayette, on the C., I. & L. (Monon) Railway.

ORIGIN AND CHARACTER OF THE WATER.—This spring has long been a favorite resort for the many visitors to the famous Tippecanoe Battle Ground. It emerges from the bank of Burnett's Creek and the ground over which the water flows is coated with an ocherous deposit of oxide of iron. The flow is a plentiful one and the temperature 53° F. The water is of a mild chalybeate character and very agreeable to the palate. At a short distance up the creek there is a second spring of a similar character.

It would be difficult to find a place better adapted for a sanitarium than the region near this spring. The Battle Ground itself is a place of much interest, which is yearly visited by many. It has beautiful surrounding scenery, especially along the old Tippecanoe trail, on the west bank of the Wabash River between the Battle Ground and Lafayette. Here there are many picturesque hills covered with fine groves of native timber, with pleasant roadways for riding and driving, winding among them. Excellent opportunities for bathing would be afforded, not only with the mineral water, but also in the waters of Burnett's Creek and the Wabash River. The sulphur water from the paper mill well in South Lafayette could be easily piped to such a sanitarium, thus affording a combination of waters of exceeding merit.

VANDERBURGH COUNTY.

FRITZLAR MINERAL WELL.

WATER=*Alkaline-saline-chalybeate.*

LOCATION.—On the west bank of Pigeon Creek, in the western part of Evansville, a city of 60,000 population, situated on the Ohio River, 122 miles by rail below Louisville. Seven railways enter the city, furnishing easy transportation facilities in all directions. Electric cars run within two blocks of the well.

ORIGIN AND CHARACTER OF THE WATER.—Like the great majority of flowing wells in the State, this one was bored for gas in 1887. The total depth of the bore was 1,830 feet. The vein of mineral water was struck at 1,030 feet, presumably in the Niagara limestone. The surface of the bore is 30 feet above low water mark in Pigeon Creek, and the water bubbles up with great force through a five-inch casing. An analysis, by Wm. Fritsch, a chemist of Evansville, showed the mineral ingredients of the water to be as follows:

ANALYSIS OF WATER FROM THE FRITZLAR MINERAL WELL, EVANSVILLE, INDIANA.

Grains per U. S. Gallon.

Sodium chloride (NaCl)	2227.120
Calcium sulphate (CaSO₄)	32.704
Calcium carbonate (CaCO₃)	220.188
Magnesium carbonate (MgCO₃)	64.816
Iron oxide (Fe₂O₃)	20.35
Aluminum oxide (Al₂O₃)	6.172
Silica (SiO₂)	3.088
Total solids	2574.438

The water as it issues is very salty, too much so for internal use without dilution. The temperature is 72° F. It has purgative qualities when taken inwardly. Externally it is much used for skin diseases, catarrh, etc. It is claimed that one gallon of the water yields a little over one-half pound of salt by evaporation. The owner, Dr. Wm. Cluthe, of Tell City, Indiana, was, in September, 1901, making arrangements for putting in an evaporating plant for securing the salt.

IMPROVEMENTS.—A bath house with facilities for summer bathing only has been erected a few rods from the well. Two cement lined pools are in use. The principal one is 90x45 feet in size; the water being eight feet in depth at one end and three feet at the other. The water passes by separate pipes into each pool, and a constant current passes from the pools into Pigeon Creek. Numerous bath houses for dressing surround the pools. In the bath house proper there are facilities for shower baths and mineral baths, there being 21 well equipped bath rooms. There are no means of heating the water, so that the place is kept open only during the summer months. It is well patronized by the citizens of Evansville; the income being $1,800 to $2,000 from bathing privileges and rent of suits during the season.

SEVENTH AVENUE MINERAL WELL.

WATER = *Alkaline-chalybeate-sulphuretted.*

LOCATION.—On Seventh Avenue, Evansville, in front of the Indiana Stove Works, and belonging to that corporation.

ORIGIN AND CHARACTER OF THE WATER.—This well, the water of which is much used locally, is but 185 feet in depth and the water is raised by a pump. An analysis of the water by Mr. Wm. Fritsch resulted as follows:

ANALYSIS OF WATER FROM THE SEVENTH AVENUE WELL, EVANSVILLE, INDIANA.

Grains per U. S. Gallon.

Carbonate of iron ($FeCO_3$) and alumina (Al_2O_3)	8.001
Calcium carbonate ($CaCO_3$)	12.96
Calcium sulphate ($CaSO_4$)	.123
Magnesium carbonate ($MgCO_3$)	2.76
Sodium chloride ($NaCl$)	3.08
Silica (SiO_2)	1.235
Total solids	28.159

Gases.	*Cu. In.*
Sulphuretted hydogen (H_2S)	1.224
Ammonia (NH_3)	0.108

In September the water as pumped had a temperature of 63° F. and a distinct, though not strong, odor and taste of hydrogen sulphide.

WILLARD' MARKET WELL.

WATER = *Saline-chalybeate.*

LOCATION. — On the Willard or Lower Market Square, in the western portion of Evansville.

ORIGIN AND CHARACTER OF THE WATER.—The water of this well is also much used locally. The well is 187 feet deep and the water is raised by a pump. An analysis by Mr. Fritsch resulted as follows:

ANALYSIS OF WATER FROM WILLARD MARKET WELL, EVANSVILLE, INDIANA.

Grains per U. S. Gallon.

Carbonate of iron ($FeCO_3$) and alumina (Al_2O_3)............ 2.76
Calcium sulphate ($CaSO_4$)................................46.28
Magnesium carbonate ($MgCO_3$)......................... 7.252
Sodium chloride ($NaCl$)................................ 7.88
Silica (SiO_2).. .500
_____
Total solids.......................................64.672

VIGO COUNTY.

EXCHANGE MINERAL WELL.

WATER = *Thermal...Alkaline-saline-sulphuretted.*

LOCATION.—Three blocks southeast of the Union Railway Station at Terre Haute, a city of 40,000 population, situated on the Wabash River, 73 miles west of Indianapolis, 167 miles east of St. Louis and 178 miles south of Chicago. Nine railways make the city easy of access from all directions. Electric lines penetrate all portions of the city, and pass within two squares of the well.

ORIGIN AND CHARACTER OF THE WATER.—This well has a depth of 1,865 feet. The mineral water comes from a limestone struck at about 1,800 feet. Gas enough issues with the water to heat the latter for bathing purposes, and partially heat a large bath house. The output of mineral water is estimated at 100 gallons per minute. A portion of the surplus water not needed in the bath house, is used on a water wheel to pump fresh water from a driven well.

An analysis of the mineral water, made by Dr. W. A. Noyes, of the Rose Polytechnic, gave the following result:

ANALYSIS OF THE WATER FROM THE EXCHANGE ARTESIAN WELL, TERRE HAUTE, INDIANA.

Grains per U. S. Gallon.

Calcium chloride (CaCl$_2$)............................... 12.941
Calcium sulphide (CaS)................................ 1.197
Calcium sulphate (CaSO$_4$)............................. 0.257
Calcium bi-carbonate (CaH$_2$(CO$_3$)$_2$)................. 19.927
Magnesium chloride (MgCl$_2$)........................... 11.055
Magnesium bi-carbonate (MgH$_2$(CO$_3$)$_2$)............. 15.344
Potassium chloride (KCl).............................. 3.625
Sodium chloride (NaCl)................................301.258
Silica (SiO$_2$)... 0.706
Alumina (Al$_2$O$_3$)....................................... 0.053
Iron bi-carbonate.................................... 0.035

Total solids.......................................366.398

Cu. In.

Hydrogen sulphide gas (free)......................... 12.017

Besides the above, traces of strontium chloride, lithium chloride, borax, calcium phosphate, sodium iodide and sodium bromide occur in the water.

The water, as it issues from the well, has a constant temperature of 80° F. It is therefore to be classed as a thermal water, and is one of the few examples of such waters occurring in the State. The amount of hydrogen sulphide present is not sufficient to lessen the very agreeable sweetish-saline taste which the water possesses, though the high temperature renders it somewhat less palatable than it would otherwise be. Testimonials from many persons attest the value of the water for the cure of rheumatic affections, skin diseases, indigestion, catarrh, etc.

IMPROVEMENTS.—"The Exchange Artesian Mineral Springs Bath House and Swimming Pool" is the name of a commodious, finely equipped bath house, built of brick and stone, which has been connected with the Exchange well for a number of years. It contains 34 bath rooms, with all necessary appliances; facilities for vapor and Turkish baths; a swimming pool 66x75 feet in size, the water being 10 feet deep at one side, and three feet at the other. A large laundry and drying room, engines, boilers, etc., occupy the basement. Hotel accommodations are lacking in the building but can be readily secured elsewhere in the city. The present proprietor, Mr. David Bronson, is quite old and wishes to dispose of the property. He has, it is claimed, $40,000 invested. A tract of land adjoining, well suited for the location of a hotel and park, can be secured for a reasonable sum. The bath house is open the year round, and is well patronized by the citizens of Terre Haute.

MAGNETIC MINERAL WELL.

WATER = *Thermal...Alkaline-saline-sulphuretted.*

LOCATION.—At the foot of Walnut Street, Terre Haute, within a short distance of the Wabash River. An electric street car line runs within two blocks of the well.

ORIGIN AND CHARACTER OF THE WATER. — This well was sunk about 1868, in search of oil, to a depth of 1,912 feet. A strong flow of mineral water was developed at about 1,800 feet, in probably the same stratum as that from which the water of the Exchange Well is obtained, and two other veins at 1,840 and 1,912 feet, respectively. All three were allowed to mix, and the flow from them approximates 180 gallons per minute of a thermal water, having a constant temperature of 80½° F. An analysis of the water by Dr. W. A. Noyes, showed the mineral salts present to be as follows:

ANALYSIS OF WATER FROM THE MAGNETIC MINERAL WELL, TERRE HAUTE, INDIANA.

Grains per U. S. Gallon.

Calcium chloride ($CaCl_2$)	16.297
Calcium sulphide (CaS)	2.078
Calcium sulphate ($CaSO_4$)	0.274
Calcium bi-carbonate ($CaH_2(CO_3)_2$)	21.942
Magnesium chloride ($MgCl_2$)	13.945
Magnesium bi-carbonate ($MgH_2(CO_3)_2$)	16.445
Potassium chloride (KCl)	3.957
Sodium chloride (NaCl)	347.734
Silica (SiO_2)	0.718
Alumina (Al_2O_3)	0.175
Total solids	423.565

Cu. In.

Hydrogen sulphide	15.259

In addition to the salts given above, traces of strontium chloride, calcium phosphate, lithium chloride, borax, sodium iodide, sodium bromide and methane or marsh gas occur in the water. The water from this well is mildly aperient, alterative and tonic. It closely resembles the water from the Exchange Well in taste and odor, and has proven very beneficial for the same diseases. It is used extensively in the sanitarium connected with the well, and is also sold quite extensively, bringing 20 cents a gallon in kegs, or $4.00 a barrel when shipped.

IMPROVEMENTS.—A sanitarium and bath house was erected in 1875, and remodeled and refurnished in 1889. It is open all the year. It contains 35 private bath rooms and good facilities for Turkish, vapor and mud baths. Connected with it is a natatorium or swimming pool, 40x60 feet in size, in which the water ranges from four to seven and a half feet in depth. This is not under roof, yet the water never freezes, as a constant stream flows through it from the well. It is open four months in the year. Both the sanitarium and natatorium are under the charge of A. P. Conant, a gentleman who has had long experience in the business. Both deserve and are receiving a good patronage not only from the citizens of Terre Haute, but from those of many other parts of the Wabash Valley.

TERRE HAUTE GAS COMPANY'S ARTESIAN WELL.

WATER=*Thermal...Saline-sulphuretted* (?).

LOCATION.—Within a few rods of the Wabash River, near the foot of Swan Street, one and one-half squares below the Magnetic Mineral Well above described.

ORIGIN AND CHARACTER OF THE WATER.—This well was drilled in 1889 for gas or oil. It is the only well in and about Terre Haute which has been sunk to the Trenton limestone. According to Martin N. Diall, who superintended the boring, the total depth of the bore is 2,930 feet. The top of Trenton was reached at 2,680 feet and that formation was pierced 250 feet. Between 1,800 and 1,900 feet, a strong vein of sulphur water was encountered, and 50 feet in the Trenton limestone, a second vein of water, rich in hydrogen sulphide gas and very black with particles of iron sulphide, was also developed. When the casing of the well was pulled, these veins mixed and are now flowing from the well with a very strong pressure and an output of 250 gallons or more per minute. A test was made soon after the well was finished which showed that the water would rise 85 feet above the surface and overflow in a four and a half inch pipe. The flow has decreased little, if any, since. A large amount of hydrogen sulphide gas (estimated by Mr. Diall at about 50,000 cubic feet per 24 hours) also issues with the water. This coats everything near by with a white coating of free sulphur. The water has a temperature of 81½° F. The taste is sweetish-saline-sulphuretted, not disagreeable after a little experience. No use is made of the water, and the site is an excellent one for a large medical sanitarium, operated under the management of an experienced physician.

ROSE ARTESIAN WELL.

WATER = *Alkaline-saline-sulphuretted.*

LOCATION.—Near the northwest corner of Eighth Street and Wabash Avenue, back of the present "Terre Haute House."

ORIGIN AND CHARACTER OF THE WATER.—A bore was made by Chauncey Rose on the ground mentioned in 1865: It reached a depth of 1,793 feet, passing through three horizons of salt water in the carboniferous rocks, and one or more in the sub-carboniferous. In the lower 100 feet of the well a strong flow of sulphur water was obtained. It is thought that the well terminated near the base of the sub-carboniferous limestone. The water rose to a considerable elevation above the surface, with an irregular pulsating flow, and was mixed with gas emitting a strong odor of sulphuretted hydrogen, and leaving on the reservoir a deposit of sulphur. An analysis of the water made by Dr. J. G. Pohle showed its mineral constituents to be as follows:

ANALYSIS OF WATER FROM ROSE ARTESIAN WELL, TERRE HAUTE, INDIANA.

Grains per U. S. Gallon.

Sodium chloride ($NaCl$)	316.000
Magnesium chloride ($MgCl_2$)	6.428
Calcium chloride ($CaCl_2$)	4.816
Potassium chloride (KCl)	1.232
Sodium bi-carbonate ($Na_2H_2(CO_3)_2$)	.520
Calcium sulphate ($CaSO_4$)	2.325
Magnesium bi-carbonate ($MgH_2(CO_3)_2$)	6.420
Calcium bi-carbonate ($CaH_2(CO_3)_2$)	25.026
Silicic acid (SiO_2) and alumina (Al_2O_3)	1.200
Nitrogenous organic matter	1.100
Total	365.067

Besides the salts mentioned, traces of magnesium bromide, calcium sulphate and calcium phosphate were present.

By comparison it will be seen that the analyses of the waters from the Rose, the Exchange and the Magnetic Mineral wells are very similar, and there is little doubt but that the water from all three had a common source in a stratum of limestone lying at approximately 1,800 feet below the surface.

But little use was ever made of the water from the Rose Well. It was finally plugged, and remains thus at the present time.

WABASH COUNTY.

WHITE'S INSTITUTE ARTESIAN WELL.

WATER = *Chalybeate.*

LOCATION.—By the side of the public road in the valley of Treaty Creek, three-quarters of a mile southeast of White's Institute; on the southeast quarter Section 31 (27 N., 7 E.). Six miles southeast of Wabash, the county seat, a city of 8,700 population, situated on the Wabash River, at the junction of the Michigan Division of the Big Four and Wabash railways, 88 miles northeast of Indianapolis, and 30 miles southwest of Fort Wayne.

ORIGIN AND CHARACTER OF THE WATER.—A well, sunk for gas in 1887 to a depth of 1,000 feet, developed in the Niagara limestone at a depth of 240 feet a strong vein of mineral water. In November, 1902, the water was flowing from an iron pipe, four feet above the ground, at the rate of 40 gallons a minute. It was clear and sparkling, and had a temperature of 56° F. No odor of hydrogen sulphide gas was detected. Objects about the well were, however, coated with the brownish red precipitate of carbonate of iron, and the characteristic taste of that salt was present. No analysis of the water has been made. It is often brought into Wabash by the barrel and is used for stomach troubles.

The well is located near the edge of a fine piece of woodland, which is much frequented by picnic parties, the drive from Wabash being in many places very picturesque.

WARREN COUNTY.

INDIANA MINERAL SPRINGS.

WATER = *Neutral.*

LOCATION.—On the northwest quarter of the southeast quarter of Section 23 (22 N., 8 W.), four and one-half miles northwest of Attica, a city of 3,100 population, situated on the Wabash River, and at the junction of the Wabash Railway and the Brazil Division of the C. & E. I. Railway; 21 miles west of Lafayette, 118 miles south of Chicago and 87 miles northwest of Indianapolis. Conveyances from the springs meet all trains. Reduced rate round trip tickets on the railways include transportation fees from Attica to the springs and return. Postoffice, Kramer. Telegraph and telephone office in the hotel.

ORIGIN AND CHARACTER OF THE WATER.—Three springs, emerge from the base of a prettily wooded ridge whose crest is 50 feet above the level of their point of issue. The main spring is 200 yards from the hotel, the others 75 yards further. Well-like pits have been sunk about their openings. In the pit of the main spring an iron cylinder, 12 feet in length and eight feet in diameter, has been sunk. In the other two, stone cylinders of smaller size retain the water. There is no overflow from any of the springs. On August 6, 1901, the water in each was about three feet in depth. Iron pipes connect the springs with tanks in the hotel, and the supply is largely pumped to these tanks and from them finds its way to the bath house, and to the drinking fountain in the hotel office. The total output from the three springs is estimated at 20 gallons per minute.

The water when dipped up from the springs, is clear, sparkling with bubbles of carbonic acid gas, and tasteless. The temperature is 53° F. The only quantitative analysis of the water of these springs available was made for Wm. Cameron, the former owner, by Dr. Stockder, and published by Dr. A. C. Peale.* It shows the composition of the water to be as follows:

ANALYSIS OF WATER FROM INDIANA MINERAL SPRINGS.

	Grains per U. S. Gallon.
Calcium bi-carbonate ($CaH_2(CO_3)_2$)	17.696
Calcium sulphate ($CaSO_4$)	1.850
Sodium chloride ($NaCl$)	.331
Magnesium oxide (MgO)	6.005
Silica (SiO_2)	.964
Total solids	26.846

	Cu. In.
Carbonic acid gas	3.836

This analysis shows a very pure ordinary spring water which may be classed as slightly alkaline or neutral.

A qualitative analysis made by J. B. Russell, of Detroit, Michigan, in 1893, showed the presence of the following:

Bases.	Acid Radicals.
Magnesium.	Carbonic.
Sodium.	Hydrochloric.
Calcium.	Sulphuric.
Lithium.	
Potassium (traces).	

	Grains.
Total solid residue from one U. S. gallon	20.21

*Bulletin 32, U. S. Geological Survey, 1886, p. 141. The figures given by Peale are " parts in 100,000." These have been reduced to grains per U. S. gallon by multiplying by .583·

PLATE XVIII.

HOTEL AND BATH HOUSE AT INDIANA MINERAL SPRINGS, WARREN COUNTY, INDIANA.

(Bath House on the Left.)

The water is sold under the name of "Magno-Lithia" water. It is shipped to consumers in five-gallon glass bottles, the price per bottle being $1.50 at the springs. It is served at meals in the hotel and is an excellent table water.

At the foot of the slope, just below the springs, is a large deposit of muck or black mud, formed of decayed vegetation. Into this deposit the seepage from the springs, before they were improved, had found its way for an indefinite time. This mud is excavated and used in the bath room connected with the hotel in giving mud baths; after using, it is carted back and allowed to remain in or near its original resting place for a period, after which it is reused. I secured samples of this muck from a place where the supply of the day before had been gotten out for the bath room, and had them analyzed by Dr. W. A. Noyes, of Terre Haute. The results of this analysis are herewith given:

ANALYSIS OF MUD FROM INDIANA MINERAL SPRINGS.

	Per Cent.
Silica (sand) (SiO_2)	12.76
Carbon dioxide (CO_2)	0.22
Ferrous oxide (FeO)	0.85
Alumina (Al_2O_3)	2.95
Lime (CaO)	1.60
Magnesia (MgO)	0.44
Potash (K_2O)	0.83
Soda (NaCl)	0.27
Hygroscopic moisture	9.10
Combustible matter (decomposed vegetation) and water of constitution	70.98
Total	100.00

"In addition to the above, minute traces of phosphoric acid (P_2O_5), manganese oxide (MnO), and lithia (Li_2O) were present. The amount of lithia was so small that it could only be found by a careful spectroscopic examination."—*Noyes.*

The analysis shows that the deposit is largely muck, and in every way similar to thousands of others which occur in the marshes and about the lakes of northern Indiana.

IMPROVEMENTS.—A large three-story hotel, with accommodations for 150 guests, stands just west of the springs. Connected with it is one of the finest bath houses in the State, erected and especially equipped for giving the famous "mud baths" for which the resort has become noted in recent years. If necessary 200 such baths can be given daily. In giving the bath, the mud is heated by steam until it has reached a high temperature. Cold mud is then mixed with the hot until the latter is about 98° F. This is then applied by an attendant to the affected parts—the whole body if required—in the form of a poultice. From 30 to 50 minutes is required for the mud bath, when the patient passes under a shower bath and remains until all traces o' the mud are removed. He is then placed in a porcelain tub fillet with water from the springs, for a soaking, after which comes a refreshing rubbing by the attendant, who often uses salt as a skin tonic. After this the patient goes to the cooling room where another rubbing with alcohol is given if required. Wonderful cures of rheumatism and skin diseases are claimed to be made by these hot mud baths, and the claims are borne out by many testimonials published in the advertising sheets of the company.

The grounds about the hotel are ample, and contain many trees and shrubs. Billiard rooms, bowling alleys, tennis courts, music rooms, dancing halls, etc., furnish plentiful means of recreation and amusement.

HUNTER MINERAL SPRING.'.
WATER = *Neutral.*

LOCATION.—Five miles northwest of Attica, on the southeast quarter of the nor'' st quarter of Section 23 (22 N., 8 W.), one-fourth mile northwest of the Indiana Mineral Springs above described. Conveyances meet all trains at Attica. Telegraph and telephone service in the office of the hotel. Postoffice, Kramer.

ORIGIN AND CHARACTER OF THE WATER.—A spring flowing about 15 gallons per minute issues from the foot of a high, wooded bluff. The water is clear, odorless and tasteless. According to Dr. W. H. Dinsmore, the physician in charge, it contains 10.86 grains of mineral matter per U. S. gallon. Of this amount calcium bi-carbonate comprises 4.5 grains, calcium sulphate 1.5 grains, and potassium sulphate .86 of a grain. The remaining four grains are composed of magnesium carbonate, sodium chloride and silica. It is a simple alkaline water of great purity. Its temperature is 51° F. It is pumped through pipes to the fountain in the office of the hotel, and to tanks for use in the bath rooms. It also flows through a pipe to a point some 50 feet from the spring, where it issues in a drinking fountain.

The water is sold for shipment at $1.00 per five-gallon bottle. This does not include the price of receptacle, which, if desired, can be returned free by express.

IMPROVEMENTS.—A hotel with accommodations for 65 people occupies a commanding site on the crest of the hill, 110 feet above Pine

PLATE XIX.

ROOM IN BATH HOUSE AT INDIANA MINERAL SPRINGS, WARREN COUNTY, INDIANA.

Creek Valley. The view from the grounds over this valley is a magnificent one for Indiana.

Connected with the hotel are well equipped bath rooms, where mud baths are a specialty. The mud or muck is hauled from a point a mile or two distant. These baths are given under the guidance of an experienced physician, each case being diagnosed, and the temperature of the bath, length of time to be taken, etc., governed by the physical condition of the patient.

There are fine roads for driving, riding and cycling about Hunter's Springs; also beautiful grounds for field sports and good fishing in adjacent streams. The place is to be commended to those who are suffering from diseases which a plentiful supply of pure water or an application of hot mud will benefit and who are seeking a quiet retreat in a picturesque region.

KICKAPOO MAGNETIC SPRING.

WATER = *Alkaline.*

LOCATION.—On the land of J. B. Lebo, near Kickapoo, a station on the Brazil Division of the C. & E. I. Railway, three miles northeast of Attica, and 115 miles south of Chicago. Postoffice, Kickapoo.

ORIGIN AND CHARACTER OF THE WATER.—A spring of clear water wells up in a valley, on either side of which hills rise to a height of 60 or more feet. Between these hills run picturesque ravines, whose precipitous walls, composed, in some places, of soapstone, in others of gray or brown sandstone, show, by their transverse markings, the course of the ancient river as it flowed in torrents down the hillsides from the stranded and rapidly melting icebergs, during the glacial period of our world's history. Within short distances of the spring are to be seen several beautiful cataracts, from 30 to 100 feet in height, as the purling streams of this region are hurled from the precipitous bluffs over which they flow on their way to the Wabash River, a mile or two distant.

It is said that the principal spring was discovered by Kickapoo Indians as early as June, 1750. The water was analyzed in 1885 by H. A. Huston, of Purdue University, Assistant State Chemist, with the following results:

ANALYSIS OF WATER FROM KICKAPOO MAGNETIC SPRINGS, WARREN COUNTY, INDIANA.

Grains per U. S. Gallon.

Calcium carbonate (CaCO₃)................................12.35

Magnesium carbonate (MgCO₃)......................... 5.38

Ferrous carbonate (FeCO₃)............................. 0.05

Silica (SiO₂)... 0.68

Sodium sulphate (Na₂SO₄)............................. 0.99

Sodium carbonate (Na₂CO₃)........................... 0.36

Organic and volatile matter........................... 4.61

Total solids..24.42

The flow of water from this spring is about 1,500 gallons per hour, having a temperature of 50° F.

The water is a very good antacid and diuretic. It is remarkable on account of its containing no chlorides, a fact which may render its use of importance in certain disturbed conditions of the stomach. It is sold in bottles holding five gallons at $2.25. A limited number of persons can secure accommodations at the farm house near the spring. There is also a bath house which is open during the summer months.

WARRICK COUNTY.

DE GONIA SPRINGS.

WATER = *Alkaline-saline-chalybeate.*

LOCATION.—On the northwest quarter of Section 27 (6 S., 7 W.), one-fourth mile south of De Gonia, a station on the Evansville Branch of the St. Louis Division of the Southern Railway, 22 miles east of Evansville. A rate of one and one-third fare, good for 30 days, is made over the Southern to parties visiting the springs. Hacks meet all trains during the season. Postoffice, De Gonia Springs.

ORIGIN AND CHARACTER OF THE WATER.—The water at De Gonia Springs is very similar to that at McCullough's Spring, near Oakland City, and Coats' Springs, Pike County, both of which are described on previous pages. It occurs in a well 12 feet in depth. In this the water stands between seven and eight feet deep, the supply being constant at all seasons. It was reported by J. G. Ford, the proprietor, in 1901, that with two hand pumps and a man in the well to dip with a bucket, he finally succeeded in reducing the water so that the bottom could be seen and the well thoroughly cleaned. According to his report, the bottom of the well is in white clay, no rock or shale being found. A second spring, 200 feet west, has water of the same character, but is little used. A well sunk 20 feet through loess and clay at the back of the hotel, produces a very "hard water," which is free from the bitter taste of that at the "Spring."

The only analysis of the mineral water available was that published by A. C. Peale, in 1886.* The name of the chemist is not given, but it was probably made by Dr. T. C. Van Nuys, formerly chemist at Indiana University.

ANALYSIS OF WATER FROM SPRING NO. 1, DE GONIA SPRINGS.

Grains per U. S. Gallon.

Calcium carbonate (CaCO₃)...........................	16.00
Ferrous carbonate (FeCO₃)...........................	4.00
Sodium sulphate (Na₂SO₄)...........................	25.00
Potassium sulphate (K₂SO₄)...........................	7.00
Magnesium sulphate (MgSO₄)...........................	56.00
Calcium sulphate (CaSO₄)...........................	4.00
Calcium phosphate (Ca₃(Po₄)₂)...........................	2.00
Calcium chloride (CaCl₂)...........................	4.00
Silica (SiO₂)...........................	3.00
Total solids...........................	121.00

Cu. In.

Carbonic acid gas...........................	8.02

The water, when pumped, has a temperature of 62° F. It is free from the odor of hydrogen sulphide or other gas. The taste is quite bitter and astringent. When boiled, a brownish-white sediment sinks to the bottom, which removes the skin from the tongue.

The water is said to be very beneficial in diseases of the bowels and kidneys, dyspepsia, ague and skin diseases.

IMPROVEMENTS.—A frame hotel, containing 44 furnished rooms, is located a short distance from the well, and is open from June 1st to October. The grounds are spacious and well shaded. There are no facilities for baths and but few for amusement, other than walking or driving. The springs are well patronized during the season, the water having an excellent reputation among the citizens of Evansville and surrounding towns.

ASH IRON SPRINGS.

WATER = *Alkaline-saline-chalybeate.*

LOCATION.—Five miles east of Boonville, on the southwest quarter Section 34 (6 S., 7 W.). One mile south of De Gonia Springs, a station on the "Air Line" Railway, 22 miles east of Evansville, and 98 miles west of Louisville.

*Bulletin 32, U. S. Geological Survey, 1886, p. 138.

ORIGIN AND CHARACTER OF THE WATER.—These springs are three in number, situated a few rods apart on the western slope of a prettily wooded knoll which rises 20 or more feet above the surrounding plain. Formerly the waters sceped from the side of the knoll. In the present site of the main spring a hole was dug, into which part of a hollow black gum tree was sunk. At present the "springs" are wells, eight to twelve feet in depth, from which the water is raised by pumps. There is a plentiful supply of the water, the temperature of which, when pumped, is 63° F. It is of the same general class as the water at De Gonia Springs, saline-acidulous, chalybeate, bitter and astringent. No analysis was available. Circulars, issued by the company formerly operating the springs, state that the principal constituents are iron, lime, magnesia, silica, carbonic acid, sulphuric acid and chloridic acid, and claim the water to be a "valuable specific for the cure of rheumatism, diarrhea, effects of alcoholism and chronic diseases." It is claimed by persons living in the vicinity that the waters of both Ash Iron and De Gonia springs are a certain cure for hog cholera.

HISTORY AND IMPROVEMENTS.—The Ash Iron Springs are said to have been well known to the Indians, who visited them when suffering from any one of many ailments. "About fifty years ago the late James Ash became the owner of the farm upon which the springs are located. At that early day the waters had a local reputation, and were used by the neighboring farmers in the treatment of chronic cases. Mr. Ash was in time compelled to erect an addition to his farm house in order to accommodate the increasing demand of those who desired to board at the springs and drink the water. The "hotel" was enlarged from time to time to meet the requirements of his patrons, and Mr. Ash refused many large offers from parties who desired to purchase his property. The buildings were poor and constructed of rough boards, to which an annual coat of whitewash was applied. The fare was of the substantial kind that "sticks to the ribs." Amusements were limited, baths unknown.

On the death of Mr. Ash the springs property was sold at commissioners' sale. In the spring of 1897 a company was organized to take charge of the property and erect buildings suitable to the reputation of the waters. A large three-story hotel and bath house was erected and handsomely equipped on the knoll above the springs. Separate buildings for use as bowling alleys, electric light plant, dancing halls, etc., were constructed. The place was opened, and for three seasons was well patronized, when the hotel was destroyed by fire. The other buildings are still standing and the water is at present unused. The site is an excellent one for a large sanitarium, with many necessary improvements already on hand.

FAIRVIEW SPRINGS.

WATER = *Saline-chalybeate.*

LOCATION.—One mile northeast of Boonville, the county seat, a town of 3,000 inhabitants, situated on the Evansville branch of the Southern Railway, 17 miles east of Evansville. Conveyances meet all trains during the season, which lasts from June 1st to October.

ORIGIN AND CHARACTER OF THE WATER.—One natural spring and two wells furnish the water at this resort. The spring issues from the side of a knoll 150 yards southeast of the hotel. The flow is small, the water very clear, with the bitter, astringent taste which characterizes the acidulous chalybeate waters of this region. At times a white deposit of ferrous sulphate (copperas) is found on the earth around the opening of the spring. The temperature of the water is 66° F.

The shallower of the two wells produces a water less strongly charged with iron sulphate and containing more magnesia. It is nine feet in depth, with five feet of water within, and is located a few rods south of the hotel. The temperature of the water is 64° F., and the taste that of Epsom salt (magnesium sulphate).

The second well is 40 feet in depth and six feet in diameter. It was dug through fossiliferous limestone and black shale for about 32 feet, then through seven feet of blue clay to another limestone. The water is highly charged with carbonate of iron, but contains little or no sulphur or magnesium.

IMPROVEMENTS.—A good hotel and bath house, with accommodations for 40 guests, is run in connection with the springs. The grounds belonging to the property are ample, and contain many fine forest trees and much shrubbery. A small artificial lake furnishes facilities for rowing and fishing, while croquet and tennis grounds supply other modes of amusement.

WASHINGTON COUNTY.

UNDERWOOD MINERAL WELL.

WATER=*Saline.*

LOCATION.—On the land of J. W. Underwood, Section 26 (4N., 3 E.), 13 miles north of Salem, the county seat, a town of 2,000 population, situated on the C., I. & L. (Monon) Railway, 282 miles southeast of Chicago, 41 miles northwest of Louisville. The nearest railway station is Medora, seven miles north, on the B. & O. S.-W. Railway. Postoffice, Vallonia, R. F. D.

ORIGIN AND CHARACTER OF THE WATER.—A well 19 feet in depth was sunk about 1870, through clay, gravel and blue mud into a shale from which the water is derived. The well is located in rather low ground, wooded ridges rising 10 to 30 feet on each side. The water stands 10 feet deep in the well, and when raised by a wooden pump has a temperature of 58° F. While free from the odor of hydrogen sulphide it has a distinct but slight sulphur-saline taste. A rather heavy whitish efflorescence on the ground below the well, and on rocks removed and thrown to one side when the well was dug, was pronounced by T. W. Smith, a chemist, of Indianapolis, to be aluminum silicate. This efflorescence was noticed before the well was sunk, and was the principal cause of its being dug. A partial analysis of the water made in May, 1875, by a Cincinnati chemist, resulted as follows:

QUALITATIVE ANALYSIS OF WATER FROM UNDERWOOD MINERAL WELL, WASHINGTON
COUNTY, INDIANA.

Bases	*Acid Radicals.*
Sodium.	Sulphuric.
Potassium.	Hydrochloric.
Calcium.	Carbonic.
Magnesium.	Phosphoric.
Iron.	

"Of these, the sodium, calcium and magnesium among the metals and the sulphuric and hydrochloric of the acids are the most abundant. The carbonic acid is less abundant. The iron and potassium are present only in very small proportion. The phosphoric acid was found only in traces. Among the more soluble salts, the chlorides and phosphates of sodium and magnesium exist in by far the largest quantities. Of the less soluble salts the sulphate of calcium is the most abundant; next come the carbonates of sodium and magnesium.

"The specific gravity of the water is 1.0033. It affords, upon standing, but a very slight sediment, containing a small quantity of organic matter, part of which was probably formed in the water after removal from the well as the salt contained but the merest trace.

"This water is to be classed with that of the saline springs and wells such as those of Seidlitz, Pyrmont, the Ballston Spa of Saratoga, N. Y., the St. Louis Artesian Well, etc."

The water has quite a local reputation for kidney, bladder, stomach and rheumatic troubles. It is not a cathartic or purgative. On the day of my visit to the well, October 23, 1902, a young man had driven 10 miles for a half barrel of it, to be used by his father, who was suffering from inflammation of the bladder, the water having been prescribed by a Louisville physician. It has been shipped to a number of towns and cities of southern Indiana, bringing $5.00 per barrel on board the cars.

BECK'S SULPHUR SPRINGS.

WATER =: *Saline-sulphuretted.*

LOCATION.—On the northeast quarter of Section 10 (1 N., 3 E.), six miles southwest of Salem, the county seat, and one-half mile northwest of Beck's Mill, the nearest postoffice.

ORIGIN AND CHARACTER OF THE WATER.—Three springs issue from limestone rock; two of them about 30 feet apart on opposite sides of a shallow ravine. The water of the larger spring flows horizontally from the ledge of limestone at the rate of one gallon per minute, and is collected in a cavity hollowed out in the rock. In this cavity and in the rill bearing away the overflow there were white, black and purple precipitates of salts of sulphur. The water had a distinct taste and odor of hydrogen sulphide, combined with a slight saline taste, and a temperature of 60° F. On the whole, it was very palatable.

The water of the second spring, very similar in character, wells up perpendicularly from a crevice in the limestone rock, at the rate of one-half gallon per minute.

The third spring is located one-quarter of a mile farther north, on the west bank of Mill Creek, a tributary of Blue River. The water flows about 15 feet into that stream, at the rate of about one gallon per minute. Two other springs of similar water formerly welled up in low ground 30 rods west of the first two mentioned, but their openings are now covered with mud and decayed vegetation. If deemed expedient they could probably be easily put into a suitable condition for use.

The water of all these springs has quite a local reputation for dyspepsia and stomach trouble. The region in which they are located contains several caves, and the scenery along Mill Creek is in places very romantic and pleasing.

WAYNE COUNTY.

GLEN MILLER SPRINGS.

WATER = *Chalybeate.*

LOCATION.—In Glen Miller Park, a tract of 164 acres of natural woodland lying on the eastern side of Richmond, a city of 18,500 population, situated 68 miles east of Indianapolis and 75 miles northwest of Cincinnati. Four railways enter the city, viz.: The G., R. & I., the Cincinnati and Richmond and the Columbus and Indianapolis Divisions of the Pennsylvania; also the C., R. & M.

ORIGIN AND CHARACTER OF THE WATER.—Glen Miller Park is one of the most beautiful and picturesque municipal parks in Indiana. It is just broken enough to add variety to its topography and is wooded with most of the indigenous trees and shrubs of eastern Indiana. To these natural characters have been added an artificial lake, numerous roadways, bypaths and bridges, ornamental shrubbery and flowering plants, until the whole has become a place of beauty, in which the citizens justly take great pride.

Adding not a little to the value of the park is the presence of chalybeate "springs," or rather wells, three shallow and one deep, with artesian flows, which supply an abundance of pure and wholesome drinking water to its visitors. The deep well, or "big spring," as it is called, is located in a ravine near the eastern side of the park. It was drilled to a depth of 282 feet, and a strong flow of chalybeate water rises a foot above the surface, and would rise six feet if the necessary pipe were inserted. The temperature of the water is 53° F. It tastes slightly of iron and deposits the brownish-red precipitate which characterizes a true chalybeate water.

At three other points in the park bores have been sunk to a depth of 22 feet, which yield an artesian flow of excellent chalybeate water. From one of these the water is piped into Cook's Grotto, and has a temperature of 58° F. as it issues frm the discharge pipe. The temperature of the others is a degree or two lower.

In addition to these springs producing chalybeate water there are three producing fresh water, whose temperature is 54° F. One of these has a large output, sufficient to form quite a rivulet. Bordered with willows and producing from its pellucid depths many matted masses of green watercress, this stream ripples along its sinuous bed into the lake, its presence adding much to the beauty of the park.

The waters of all these springs, both chalybeate and fresh, are much used by the citizens of Richmond, many of whom visit the park with jugs and convey a plentiful supply to their homes.

REID'S SPRING.

Water = *Alkaline-chalybeate.*

LOCATION.—On the farm of David Reid, near the center of Section 29 (14 N., 1 W.), two and one-fourth miles north of Richmond.

ORIGIN AND CHARACTER OF THE WATER.—This spring wells up on the side of a gentle slope in an oak and beech grove. A section of sewer pipe three feet in diameter has been sunk about the orifice of the spring, and a square bed of cement placed around the upper end of the pipe. In this pipe the water stands three feet in depth and flows over the mouth at the rate of five gallons per minute.

A partial analysis of the water made by Dr. J. N. Hurty showed its constituents to be as follows:

QUALITATIVE ANALYSIS OF WATER FROM REID'S SPRING.

Bases.	*Acid Radicals.*
Iron.	Carbonic.
Magnesium.	Sulphuric.
Potassium.	Silicic.
Sodium.	
Calcium.	

Total solids present, 25.2 grains per U. S. gallon.

The water is clear and sparkling with carbonic acid gas. It has had a local reputation for years, chiefly as a diuretic. Large quantities are sold in Richmond at six cents per gallon, delivered in jugs.

HAWKINS' SPRING.

Water = *Alkaline-chalybeate.*

LOCATION.—On the farm of John Hawkins, one mile northeast of the city of Richmond.

ORIGIN AND CHARACTER OF THE WATER.—A lack of time forbade a visit to this spring while gathering data for this paper. The following account is taken from the report on Wayne County by Prof. E. T. Cox, in the report of this department for 1878, pp. 213, et. seq.:

"The most important springs, in a medicinal point of view in Wayne County, are on Mr. John Hawkins' farm, just northeast of the city of Richmond. The water breaks out from the junction of the drift and the blue argillaceous shales that form the upper part of the Lower Silurian beds. There are a number of springs on the place, but Mr. Hawkins has only thought proper to enclose three with cement pipes that are about two feet in diameter. They are situated on the south side of the East Fork of White River, and about 20 feet above the bed of the stream and 60 feet below the crest of the hill, at Mr. Hawkins' residence. The springs are only a few feet apart, and arranged in the form of a triangle. The ground around is neatly paved, and the overflow of water is carried off in a paved chute. This chute is well lined with a brownish-red gelatinous precipitate of ferric oxide, which tells at once the chalybeate character of the water. There is considerable gas bubbling up from the bottom of each spring, which appears to be mainly carbonic anhydride and carbonic dioxide. No odor of sulphydric acid could be detected at the spring or in the water shipped to the laboratory for analysis.

ANALYSIS OF WATER FROM HAWKINS' MINERAL SPRING, RICHMOND, INDIANA.

Grains per U. S. Gallon.

Silicates	.158
Ferrous carbonate ($FeCO_3$)	.192
Calcium sulphate ($CaSO_4$)	11.684
Magnesium sulphate ($MgSO_4$)	1.599
Calcium bi-carbonate ($CaH_2(CO_3)_2$)	9.448
Potassium carbonate (K_2CO_3)	1.170
Sodium chloride ($NaCl$)	.333
Calcium chloride ($CaCl_2$)	.323
Total solids	24.907

Free carbolic acid, 4.302 cubic inches per U. S. gallon.

"This is a sulphatic and carbonated chalybeate water; its action is that of a mild tonic, aperient and diuretic and decided alterative. A qualitative examination of the two other springs on Hawkins' farm showed no perceptible difference in the quality of the water."

INDEX TO MINERAL WATERS OF INDIANA.

(1901 Report.)

Date Due

CPSIA information can be obtained
at www.ICGtesting.com
Printed in the USA
BVHW051212040319

541705BV00016B/746/P

9 781346 445472